UNWINDING PERFECT

One Woman's Story of Reclamation

CHRISTINE CLYNE-SPRAKER

LANDON
HAIL
PRESS

Copyright© 2024 Christine Clyne-Spraker
All Rights Reserved

This book or any portion thereof may not be reproduced or used in any manner without the express written permission of the publisher, except for the use of brief quotations in a book review.

Paperback ISBN: 978-1-959955-36-8
Hardback ISBN: 978-1-959955-37-5
Cover design by Rich Johnson, Spectacle Photo
Cover photographer: Angelli Nguyen
Cover creative direction: Brittany Barcellos
Published by Landon Hail Press

Although the author and publisher have made every effort to ensure the accuracy and completeness of information contained in this book, we assume no responsibility for errors, inaccuracies, omissions, or any inconsistency herein. Any slights on people, places, or organizations are unintentional. The material in this book is provided for educational purposes only. No responsibility for loss occasioned to any person or corporate body acting or refraining to act as a result of reading material in this book can be accepted by the author or publisher.

This book is dedicated to my imperfectly perfect family.
Never once did I not feel loved. I love you all, all the bushels.

I pay homage to the old me and to the expanded me. I celebrate each decision, because they led me here today.

CONTENTS

Foreword --- 9
Preface -- 11
PART I: FORTY YEARS IN THE MAKING -------------------- 17
Chapter 1: Shadows -- 19
Chapter 2: Family -- 22
Chapter 3: Generational Patterns: A Perfect Bubble ------------ 29
Chapter 4: Burst Bubble --- 36
Chapter 5: Life After Bear -------------------------------------- 42
Chapter 6: Fractures -- 45
Chapter 7: People-Pleasing and Religion ---------------------- 50
Chapter 8: Tammy -- 54
Chapter 9: Life Happens --- 60
Chapter 10: Imposter Syndrome ---------------------------------- 63
Chapter 11: Authenticity -- 70
Chapter 12: The Start of an Awakening ------------------------- 76
Chapter 13: A Transformative Catalyst ------------------------- 81
Chapter 14: Davie Blu --- 84
PART II: UNWINDING --------------------------------------- 93
Chapter 15: Perfectionism --------------------------------------- 95
Chapter 16: Covid -- 99

Chapter 17: Diane Von Furstenberg --------- 104

Chapter 18: Hard Conversations --------- 108

Chapter 19: Leading with Love --------- 116

Chapter 20: Signs --------- 121

Chapter 21: Sedona --------- 125

Chapter 22: Permission --------- 134

Chapter 23: Boundaries --------- 140

Chapter 24: Shapeshifting --------- 146

Chapter 25: A Message from the Earth --------- 150

Chapter 26: The Tiny House --------- 155

Chapter 27: Jane the Virgin --------- 162

Chapter 28: Cocoon --------- 172

Chapter 29: Attachment to Outcome --------- 176

Chapter 30: Healing --------- 182

Chapter 31: Loïck --------- 190

Chapter 32: Metamorphosis --------- 199

PART III: APPENDIXES --------- 202

Chakra and Visualization Meditation --------- 204

HeartMath™ --------- 214

Exercises in Self-Discovery --------- 216

Acknowledgments --------- 230

About the Author --------- 234

"You own everything that happened to you. Tell your stories. If people wanted you to write warmly about them, they should have behaved better."

—Anne Lamott

CHRISTINE CLYNE-SPRAKER

Foreword

IN THE TWISTS AND TURNS of existence, certain exceptional individuals are driven by the vigor of their spirit, by the determination of their will, by the ardor of their inspiration, and the unshakeable faith in the beat of their heart. Seeking deep meaning in their lives, they strive tirelessly to understand how to make the life of both their material dreams and their spiritual dreams come true.

Listening attentively to the sacred words that their hearts subtly whisper, they push tirelessly to achieve what their souls aspire to, even without fully grasping its precise meaning. These individuals walk in the burning fire of existence, struggling internally to gradually decipher the meaning of this innate inspiration present in each of us, often expressing the ardor of this quest called "*LIFE.*"

Some, like heroes, decide to embrace this difficult adventure—the journey toward self-evolution, transcending their own limitations to reveal and unlock unexplored treasures. Treasures that are both poignant and magnificent emerge to illuminate not only their material successes and their inner growth, but also, and above all, to realize the meaning of a free and fulfilling life.

Through the story that I have the honor to preface, we can witness the deep inner devotion that Christine demonstrated throughout her life. This journey requires deep reflection on oneself; an intense life force; a strength to love, and a power to overcome suffering; a capacity for continuous adaptation. Thus, through these book lines, we can discover a soul in full growth, on the path toward fulfillment. They reveal in an almost magical way the hidden meaning of events and circumstances, as well as the courage of its own choices. I encourage you to read this book as a witness to someone moving forward on the path to personal development, who is sharing with sincerity in order to encourage and clarify the path for everyone on their own journey.

May my few lines awaken in you the inspiration and resilience that Christine found on her path to becoming the great woman she is today.

Loïck Boulmot, Spiritual Mentor and Mystic Whisperer

Preface

"Writing, to me, is simply thinking through my fingers."
—Isaac Asimov

I'M JUST GOING TO SAY IT: Life is hard. You think you have it all figured out… or maybe you never really think that, but you act like you do… and then, well, things change. You have a spouse, you never find a spouse; you have some kids, you find out you can't have kids; you buy a home, you can't afford to buy a home; your work demands more from you than you can give, you decide to build a company, or perhaps you make the really tough decision not to have a career and be a stay-at-home parent. Whatever your situation is, my guess is the road was not paved with unicorns and rainbows.

My path sure wasn't, but from an outsider's perspective, it might look like it. I was what some might consider living a very charmed life and at the top of my game. I had been married for almost sixteen-years, had two bright and kind children, lived in a beautiful home in an affluent Denver neighborhood, and was a co-CEO of a healthcare technology company I had helped build from the ground up. My identity was wrapped around the fact that I was a business leader, a female in a male dominated industry, often the only woman at the table, and on many occasions mistaken for the secretary (which used to infuriate me). I now can laugh about it.

I worked really hard to make sure I was all things to all people and spent the last decade about as tightly wound as a spool of sewing thread. As a serial people-pleaser since childhood, I learned at a young age that my value and self-worth derived from meeting others' needs. Don't rock the boat at home, and be the easy child. Present perfect from the outside, and don't discuss difficult emotions or share vulnerabilities. Put your head down and do the work.

Ironically, all of these things served me extremely well, professionally. I became a successful medical-device sales rep early in my career (put your head down and do the work). I was likable, manageable, and promotable (present perfect from the outside, and don't discuss hard things). And, I was smart and knew how to play the game (don't rock the boat, and be the easy child). I worked hard, I thrived on accolades and recognition, and I did well.

Years later, when I got the opportunity to help build Eon, I took all of those things I had learned to be successful and wrapped them up into operating a business. Today, the business is a leading healthcare technology company and paving the way for massive shifts in how patients are managed and tracked within a healthcare system. I couldn't be prouder of what we built and the lives we have impacted.

But where these traits did not serve me well was *personally*. I was lonely and alone. My marriage had been failing for years. I was often insecure about how to connect with my children as they grew older, and in order to give to the business what it needed to become the high growth company it is today, I had to basically stop nurturing friendships. This meant less essential time invested in friends, which is necessary for healthy and flourishing friendships.

As I became busier professionally and with life in general, I increasingly became more and more sick. So much so that my hair started breaking off and falling out in 2017. And I found myself in an awful habit, constantly running from one thing to the next—whether it was work meetings, kids' activities, or house priorities, I never slowed down. I never took the time to rest. And I was never mentally present. My mind constantly averted to what was next or needed to be done or who had to be where.

In 2022, I made the incredibly painful decision to move out of our family home and into a small rental that I affectionately call the Tiny House. Being in that space allowed me the opportunity to grieve the loss of my marriage, to begin to focus on my needs, and to have some down time, helping me refocus my personal and professional priorities.

I loved the business, and I loved the team, but the company had grown so much and so quickly, it was ready for a single leader and a CEO versus the co-CEO structure that had served it so well for many years. My heart broke yet again, but I made the painful decision to resign and step away from the business. Inside, my gut was telling me there was a different and new path for me, one that would accelerate my self-actualization goals and my life's purpose, even though I had no idea what that might look like.

I went from sixty-plus-hour work weeks, full-time kid responsibilities, and constantly being on the go to being alone with zero obligations fifty percent of the time. It was indeed the hardest thing I have ever been through. But through these incredibly painful decisions, clarity and light began to seep in. I started to do some really hard self-help work. And while I had been scratching the surface of a spiritual journey for years, my sudden down time allowed me the space to fully embrace it in a whole new way.

I started writing again. At first, it was a long-form blog on topics that were cathartic to write about. Then, at the urging of some friends, a book just started to spill out of me.

As I began to share my journey of shedding my old skin—the generational patterning and conditioning that had led me to be the way I was—an inner voice urged me to keep going. To keep writing. As I verbally shared my story with more and more people, I realized there was an opportunity to help others take personal agency by stepping forward and doing their own hard work.

I think, when we are vulnerable, the disconnect between people softens. Shortens. The proverbial olive branch is extended, and an opportunity to see someone in a different way emerges. As less threatening, less scary, less different; more real, more like each other. I truly believe, if people let their guard down and take off the mask that they feel they must wear in the world, love and peace and joy could triumph.

This book is a story about my self-help journey to reclaim who I am and, inadvertently, fall in love with myself; for the first time ever. Through the book, I share some of the resources I found useful and that have since had a profound impact on my life. My hope is, through this story, someone, somewhere will feel empowered and inspired enough to choose themselves. To choose to do the hard work. To choose to unwind whatever is holding them back from stepping into the life that they desire and deserve.

CHRISTINE CLYNE-SPRAKER

PART I

FORTY YEARS IN THE MAKING

CHRISTINE CLYNE-SPRAKER

Chapter 1

Shadows

"Who looks outside, dreams; who looks inside, awakes."
—Carl Jung

I AM ONLY ONE PERSON. And I am only responsible for me. Even my sweet kids, whom I adore and love and will protect until the day I die, must make their own decisions on how to show up in the world. And while the old me would love to tell them how to do it, I'm learning that it is for them to figure out. Not for me to try to force or project my fears on.

I know I'm not alone when I say I allowed certain core wounds and familial patterning to run my never-ending inner dialogue and outer behavior. For forty-plus years, I was the people-pleaser and the suppressor of my true inner emotions. My subconscious worked very hard to project the "perfect" persona to the world, and it was exhausting. Eventually, I would come to learn that, for all of my light, I had just as much darkness within me. Darkness that I felt shameful and guilty about, so I worked very hard to hide it from myself and others. My shadows, this darkness, was scary, ugly, and unlovable. Or so I believed.

As I began my journey to heal, I had to confront my shadows, an extremely painful process. Each of us has shadows, and no one is immune from them. They are results of our family structure, community, social norms, schooling, and other conditioning that surround us, as children. Our shadows are the qualities, impulses, and emotions that we are too scared for other humans to see—most likely because we learned at a young age there is a negative consequence when we say or act a certain way. We learn to hide or suppress those natural impulses or emotions deep within ourselves, to protect us from future embarrassment, pain, criticism, negative self-talk, and other potential hurt.

Carl Jung, considered the grandfather of modern psychology, said, "The meeting with oneself is, at first, the meeting with one's own shadow. The shadow is a tight passage, a narrow door, whose painful constriction no one is spared, who goes down to the deep well. But one must learn to know oneself, to know who one is." If we allow them to be, our shadows can also be our greatest teachers.

For most of my life, I didn't understand that shadows and core wounds play such a large role in why adults behave the way they do. Both good and bad. My shadows led me to be controlling and fearful of what outcome might happen if I didn't oversee every aspect of a situation. They also led me to be a people-pleaser—scared to death of abandonment—which led to my willingness to sacrifice my inner self to avoid potential abandonment.

Compensating behaviors are a result of us simply trying to protect ourselves from the pain we felt from the traumatic childhood events we experienced. We think we are protecting ourselves by doing this, fearful that, if we act the way that led to the traumatic event, the same pain will be felt once again. We do what we can to avoid it. Ironically, most of these compensatory behaviors, emotions, thoughts, and actions are rooted in fear. Understanding the fear that drives us is critical to unwinding self-sabotaging behaviors.

The amount of energy exerted into the fear driving our behaviors is exponentially greater than taking a step back and analyzing what is really the motivator behind our actions. When we can take this step back, we become witnesses to our own inner dialogue, and through witnessing, we can begin to determine what is real and what isn't. Eventually, one can learn to release that fear, surrender, and be forever free from it.

Most of us weren't raised to know or understand this, and if someone had told me this a few years ago, I would have either laughed or been confused. I was naive to the negative and cyclical patterns in my own mind, having learned to cope by compartmentalizing emotions and events in my life.

What is lost on an older generation and seems to come so naturally to a younger generation leaves an entire middle generation, my generation, hungry for self-awareness, introspection, growth, and change. It's as scary as it gets. But for me, it has been life-changing and transformative in ways I could never have imagined.

To understand my journey to begin to choose myself, we must first start at the beginning.

Chapter 2

Family

"Storytelling reveals meaning without committing the error of defining it."

—Hannah Arendt

I WAS BORN DURING *Monday Night Football*. My parents like to tell the story of how both my dad and the doctor were watching the game and paying more attention to it than to my mom.

In their defense, I was refusing to come out. I was already sixteen days late, and my mom wasn't dilating. She was big, and she still talks about the muumuu dresses she had to wear, long before fashion had embraced making stylish maternity clothes.

My dad and the doctor had the game on in the hospital room and it was a welcomed distraction. The Houston Oilers were playing the Miami Dolphins, and from what I can tell, it wasn't much of a game. The Oilers ended up winning by three, in a 9-6 finish. But I guess, back then, you could only get football on one channel at a time; there was no streaming. It beat sitting in a hospital room with a barely laboring woman and my mom has never been a demanding person. The Pitocin was dripping, and she had an epidural, so I don't think she minded too much.

Prior to my arrival, her doctor was convinced I was a boy, so my parents planned to call me John, after my mom's father. When I finally arrived, I was bald and looked much like a boy. After initially confusing me for a boy, the doctor announced I was a healthy baby girl, and I tipped the scales at a mighty 9 pounds, 4 ounces.

The doctor performed the standard Apgar test, giving me a score of 9.9 and proudly stating, "I would give her a ten, but there is no such thing as a perfect baby."

I wonder if this impressed upon my little baby brain, subconsciously, that, "Gosh darn it, you are almost perfect. Maybe you could try a little harder..." As much as I would try to present a perfect image from that day forward, no matter what I did or how hard I tried, it would never come to be.

My parents struggled for three days with what to name me. Since John was no longer an option, they had to start thinking about girl names for the first time. My dad suggested Carla or Gail. My mom liked Jillian and wanted to call me Jill. Even my Grandma Nita thought she had the perfect name: Dee Dee. But finally, my parents agreed on Kimberly, and I was Kimberly for about ten hours. Until the staff brought me to my mom in the middle of the night to nurse, and she said it just didn't sit right.

My mom called my dad at home at 5 a.m. that morning, waking him out of a dead sleep. Oh, to be a man in the late 1970s! He agreed to Jillian. Until about 9 a.m. that same morning, when he said he just couldn't do it. He couldn't call me Jill.

So finally, after three long days in the hospital, I came home as Christine. My parents knew three people named Christine, and they liked all three of them, so that's how I became Christine. And with the agreement that they would never shorten it to Chris.

I've always been fascinated by how a name takes on an identity and how it forever plays a role in that human's life. There are stories of how job candidates will sometimes get passed over because of their name. Or how the well-intentioned name from Mom and Dad leads that child to be teased endlessly on the playground, because it mercilessly rhymes with a body part.

For me, I just flat-out have a hard time saying my name. As the recipient of speech therapy as a young kid, I just don't say it quite right. If I'm speaking fast or have had a drink, a little lisp comes out. Something about the way my mouth forms *Chris* is just a little off. It's taken a lot of practice for me to slow down and enunciate both the *Chris* and the *tine*, so it doesn't wet noodle anytime I'm introducing myself or saying my name.

I came from a very loving and kind family and had no reason to believe anything but unicorns and rainbows growing up. I had two parents who loved me dearly and three siblings whom I adored. We were not, however, a "normal" 1980s family. We were a real-world Brady Bunch and the only family I knew who was a blended family. While my mom and dad have known each other since they were eight and nine years old, their first marriages were to other people.

They had gone to church together at the First Baptist Church of Detroit and basically grew up together. My dad still likes to talk about my mom and her fitted sweaters, and how he always liked her but never had the courage to ask her out. So, instead of dating him, my mom married a good friend of my dad's, and my dad was the best man in their wedding. By the time my dad married his first wife, my mom was eight months pregnant with my sister, Kerry.

Years later, my entrepreneurial father, frustrated by the Michigan union home-painting rules that made it difficult for him to paint houses as efficiently as he knew he could, decided to leave Detroit for Denver. He took a small loan from his favorite uncle to start a painting business and made the move with his first wife. Soon after settling in Denver, they had two children together, Amy and Andrew. My mom and her first husband decided to follow them west, and he ended up getting work with my dad.

Soon after, my dad and his first wife decided to divorce, changing the dynamics of their friendships. Custody in the 1970s favored the mom, so my dad only had his children every other weekend and on the Thursday of his off weekends.

My mom's first husband was far from a saint, and serving overseas in Vietnam had only hardened him further. At some point, my mom said enough is enough and decided to divorce him. This was the mid-1970s, and other than my dad, she didn't know anyone who was divorced. She was beyond brave. She took my oldest sister, Kerry, who was six at the time, and left. They found a small apartment, got to keep the dog and the car, and my mom found a job at a local advertising company.

If she'd been born twenty years later or been raised in a less traditional family, my mom would have made a heck of a saleswoman. Her father was a storied salesman, and easy chitchat comes naturally to her. Ironically, the advertising agency position she took after her divorce would be the only job she ever held, as an adult. My mom is intelligent, a great talker, well-read, and likeable. She's also very easy on the eyes, with her big, bright blues and beautiful, long, stick-straight, blonde hair.

Since they were the only two divorced people they knew, my future parents started hanging out and spending more time together.

To this day, I can't imagine the courage it took for them to make the decision to divorce their first spouses. Especially having been raised by very conservative parents in the Baptist Church, where everyone aimed to present the perfect exterior as much as possible.

But they did find that courage, becoming sources of strength for each other. And of course, for me, I'm sure glad they did.

Growing up in a blended family, before blended families were a thing, didn't feel weird or abnormal to me. It was just my family. The hardest part about it was trying to explain to others what a half-sister or half-brother was… I didn't have any stepsiblings, so I could at least leave that part out.

Kerry is my mom's and eight years older than me; she lived with us until she went away to college. My sister Amy, who is six years older than me, and my brother Andrew, who is four years older than me, are my dad's; they were with us for dinner every Thursday and every other weekend. I so wish custody laws had been more favorable for the father back then, as we all would have loved to see them more. Everything always felt more loud, more exciting, and more fun when they were there. Plus, my brother was my first best friend, and I loved doing anything he and my dad were doing.

In early adulthood, I finally started to understand the impact our family dynamic had on the four of us. Kerry, Amy, and

Andrew were all the result of divorces and unequal custody time. (In my sister's case, probably a blessing; but as today's data shows, most of the time, children benefit from a 50/50 split.) And then there was me, the result of the "perfect" union between their parents. I was blissfully unaware of the pain and hurt each of them felt.

And it wasn't until I began therapy in my forties that I began to understand some of the deep wounds from my childhood that had also formed inside of me. Beginning to understand these early childhood wounds has helped me to better recognize much of why I am the way I am today.

For instance, I was completely unaware of generational patterns and the roles we take on, as children, within our families. We do this to help ourselves feel safe and loved. My role in my family was simple: be easygoing, and don't disrupt the apple cart. Be the stabilizer and neutralizer of conflict; don't create conflict. When the house gets chaotic and someone is fighting with someone, be the peacemaker. Intervene.

Somewhere along this path, I missed developing a sense of self. I didn't even know what my needs were, because I was so busy trying to meet everyone else's—my parents' and my siblings'. And I also learned it wasn't safe to show vulnerability. Don't share fears, don't ask tough questions, don't choose yourself over hurting others.

There is a saying that we all become our parents, and I was indeed equal parts Mom and Dad. And because neither of them had learned vulnerability, that meant feelings, tough situations, and open mistakes just weren't talked about.

In fact, I couldn't tell you how old I was when I realized my mom wasn't perfect or that she had bad days. She was always "happy" and "on." And her mother portrayed the same behavior.

And while I was, and still am, a naturally happy person, I never learned how to manage any of those harder feelings, like sadness, loneliness, and fear. So, when they popped up, I worked very hard to tuck them away in the back of my mind, instead of feeling them and working through them. When behaviors and coping mechanisms are passed down between generations, this is called generational patterning. For me, the generational patterning I grew up with created an ideal situation for me to feel as if I lived in a perfect little bubble.

Chapter 3

Generational Patterns:

A Perfect Bubble

> "Daddy! Put the top down, Daddy."
> —A fifteen-year-old Tenae Baker (aka my mom),
> in her father's red convertible Chevy Tempest

EVEN FROM A VERY YOUNG age, I knew my mom had a very special bond with her father, my Grandpa John. Grandpa John was an extraordinary man who had survived at least three near-death experiences in World War II: nearly drowning at Normandy, because he didn't know how to swim, when he jumped off of his war ship into the English Channel; a near miss by a sniper assassin; and last, surviving, but severely injured, when the French home he was bunkering in was bombed. This injury finally took him out of the war and back to his home state of Illinois to recover, where he met my grandma.

Grandpa John was a storyteller and loved to talk about how he met my grandma. The beaded fringe on her dress would move slowly back and forth with her hips as she sang in the church choir. He talked about his time as an executive in the trucking industry during the fabled 1950s and '60s union era, and how

Jimmy Hoffa once told my grandpa he had a pair of cement boots waiting for him. And he was a God-loving, God-fearing Freemason who loved my grandma fully and unconditionally.

Grandmama Nita was equally fierce, but in a submissive, mid-century-wife way. She was a stunner, with flawless creamy skin and jet-black hair. She was the kindest, most generous, while often flirtatious in just the right way, woman I have ever known. They were the epitome of a picture-perfect couple.

While my mom loved her mother very much, she had a very different relationship with her than she did with her father. Her relationship with her mother was loving and kind, but it wasn't necessarily the close bond you might imagine. In fact, my mom told me stories years later about some of the competitive actions my grandma took toward my mom.

Stories such as, if my mom had lost weight, suddenly Grandmama was losing weight. Or if my mom had success in something, Grandmama needed to show she could do it, too. It was as if my mother wasn't allowed to have her own identity, because the moment she stepped out on the highwire, her mom was right there, doing the same thing.

In hindsight, it's easy to understand how having a mother constantly competing with you might make my mom feel unsure of herself, like she had to be perfect and proper to gain acceptance from her mom. And anytime she tried to exert her own individualism, it was reigned back in.

It's also easy to see how her closest relationship was with her father and, subsequently, her younger brother, who came six years after she was born.

My grandfather's nickname for my mom growing up was "Blonde Bombshell." And yes, she was quite the bombshell. This nickname became a very important component of my mom's identity, so much so that, when her first grandchild was born, she became Bebe (BB) to her grandchildren.

In the past few years, I have come to better understand the profound impact my mom's familial relationships had on her and, subsequently, on me. And how her patterning was recreated within my childhood family structure. I easily became Daddy's little girl, loving anything he loved and feeling loved, safe, and secure in his adoration.

If anyone asked me what my favorite TV shows were in the 1980s, I would say, "Football, basketball, and the news," because those were his favorite shows. I would lie on the couch with him at night, and we would watch them together.

My mom and I were the people-pleasers in the family. I understand now how I did this to feel loved. In a family dynamic that was often chaotic, loud, disruptive, and full of noise, I protected myself by being "easy." Even if I wanted to go to dinner at Coco's, I wouldn't dare speak up, if my dad or sister had a strong restaurant preference. It was easier to let them battle it out than have an opinion.

My mom was the same way—didn't rock the boat or have strong choices about certain things. In fact, for many years, my parents would hide the liquor in our house when both of their parents came to visit. Alcohol was frowned upon by both sides, and my mom didn't want to have to admit there was alcohol in their house. It was easier to please or avoid hard conversations than to have a bottle of whiskey under the cabinet.

Also, my mom never cried. Or at least never that I saw. And she never showed anything other than being okay. She was always put together: dressed well, hair and makeup done; the example of a perfect wife. She cooked, cleaned, carpooled, PTAed, and all the things. She was an amazing mom, and I am forever grateful for the sacrifices and love she showed me.

She and my dad love each other dearly to this day, and they never fought in front of us growing up. To me, they were another perfect example of a perfect marriage, just like my grandparents. They, too, were so lovely and so perfect that I aspired to find my own true love one day, where I could be a perfect wife to my perfect husband.

A more recent realization I have come to is that I don't ever remember my mom demonstrating how to receive or to ask for what she needed. As a giver and a people-pleaser, it is easy to push one's needs to the back burner, but it is equally important to be able to ask for your needs and to receive them. This allows someone to healthily feel loved, to not settle or accept bad behaviors, and to find balance. It allows you to create healthy boundaries and to feel worthy of your needs being met. This requires a healthy sense of self and self-worth.

Although the generational patterning and conditioning also ran deep on my dad's side, he jokes that, because he was the middle child, he was mostly left alone by his parents. When I was growing up, he was a shining example of a provider, a man of faith, with great love for his family and endless lessons, like "the only free cheese is in the trap" and "a job worth doing is worth doing well." He was an entrepreneur and my inspiration to start my own first business when I was in second grade.

My dad is very loyal and taught me the importance of treating your people well, even when they might take advantage of your kindness. And when his employees or family members mistreated him, he would respond with an open heart. But, consequently, he skirted hard conversations and opportunities to create boundaries. He taught me to put your head down and pursue an outcome, sometimes to the detriment of your own needs. For me, I have come to understand that this meant letting my brain take over and to compartmentalize feelings and emotions, rather than processing them and to sometimes make the hard decision to walk away from a no-longer-healthy situation.

Being surrounded with all of this perceived perfectness in my life, I didn't really know or understand that people actually hurt. I remember the first time I saw a man panhandling on the median in my hometown. I was maybe six years-old. He had a sign that said, "Will work for food." I was broken-hearted and felt true pain. I couldn't imagine a human who had no work and no food.

And while I wouldn't allow myself to cry, I did tell my mom how concerned I was for him. She told me that, after we dropped the groceries off, we could go back and, if he was still there, give him $5. We went back, but to my little heart's great disappointment, he was gone.

Being vulnerable just wasn't a thing in my family. We didn't talk about emotions or feelings or being imperfect. If I cried, my older siblings usually would tease me and call me a baby. If I got something or did something well, they would say I was the favorite, a phrase that has carried into adulthood and caused great tension between some of my family members and me.

And I was clueless to the patterns that were forming deep within me—little dances I was learning to do with other people, to keep them happy, and to keep control of a situation, so I would feel safe and loved. So, I could predict the outcome.

The dances I learned in childhood are the same dances I have been dancing most of my adult life. Because I was loved and cared for while doing these dances as a child, I didn't realize many of my behaviors were actually detrimental to myself and those whom I loved. I knew it felt good not to rock the boat, even if that meant sweeping my emotions under the rug. I didn't know it was weird that I didn't have a real sense of self or identity. And I was a great chameleon who could fit into just about any group or situation anywhere. I now know this is called *social shapeshifting*, and social shapeshifters prioritize how people perceive and receive them over being their own authentic self, which I'll talk about a little later in this book.

My childhood, for all the love and greatness that it was, was the beginning of me learning to compartmentalize big feelings and big events. I never fully learned how to process them in a healthy way or to truly understand and know what I wanted—or how to ask for it. This was not malicious intent by my parents; they simply never had a role model to demonstrate these skills, which would have enabled them to pass these skills on to me. Because of that, none of us adequately exercised the muscles necessary to work through hard feelings.

And because I didn't understand that it was safe to not be perfect all the time, safe to take up big space, or even safe to "put people out," by choosing myself, I just never learned to be vulnerable. When you lock emotions up inside, great amounts of shame then come with it. And when you can't share your emotions like shame, because you don't feel safe being vulnerable, a vicious cycle occurs.

To compensate, I compartmentalized. By compartmentalizing my wants, my fears, my desires, my mistakes, my lessons, and my emotions, I didn't have to need, want, or feel anything. This allowed me to move forward without skipping a beat and without having to be a burden to anyone. Eventually, I became a high-functioning perfectionist.

I would just put my head down and go.

Chapter 4

Burst Bubble

"Our anxiety does not come from thinking about the future but from wanting to control it."

—Kahlil Gibran

I AM A NATURALLY optimistic and positive human being. I believe there is more good than bad in the world and that most people truly mean well. My dad modeled this, and my mom modeled constant happiness. When combined with my learned ability to compartmentalize hard emotions, I pretty much grew up in one gigantic, happy bubble. We were a middle-class White family in a safe and unremarkable suburb of Denver.

I loved my high school experience. I loved all the different groups of friends that I had, and I easily shifted between the jocks, smart kids, and stoners. I was able to walk the line between being an almost straight-A student and partying on the weekends with the "cool" kids. I equally loved learning and hated missing out on social events. My parents either didn't know or turned a blind eye to that not-so-"perfect" side of me.

At school, I was an athlete and a good, easy student. Socially, I was trying alcohol and marijuana and even smoking cigarettes.

Like many teens who experiment with identity, it was like there were two sides of me: the one I wanted my family to see, what I projected to the world, and the one who desperately wanted to fit in and feel included by my peers.

I don't remember being aware of the tension created by the duality I lived in.. I was just a normal kid who was a little rebellious and sneaky, but still meeting my parent's expectations. Disappointing them was always my biggest fear. The worst four words I could ever hear were, "We're disappointed in you."

I really didn't understand or know how much pain and hurt existed in the world. I would see the news or occasionally hear stories from friends at school, but it never really touched me. I had seemed to live this perfect little life, in a perfect little bubble, in a seemingly perfect little family. But when I was eighteen years old, that perfect bubble burst, and my life forever changed.

"Who's going to tell Christine?" I later learned was the question my friends were asking one another on the morning of April 8, 1998. It was the spring semester of my senior year of high school, and I was on top of the world. I was excited about our upcoming senior class trip, then graduating and heading to Arizona State University to study civil engineering.

But on that morning, I didn't just drop from the top of the world. I plummeted. Into a very large, very dark hole. My best friend, Jason "Bear" Haertel, had committed suicide the night before. He died the same night he had called me, asking if he could come over and hang out. The same night I had told him that he couldn't, because it was late and I was studying for a test.

To this day, I have never met a more affable human than Bear. Liked by everyone and always down for a good time, Bear was smart, funny, kind, and loyal. He loved his people fiercely and would have done anything for any of us. He was well-known for his oversized camo-colored sweatshirts, baggy jeans, and easy laugh. He was less known for his love of math and desire to become an architect. He and I shared a love for drafting and design.

The news of his death and the weeks that followed rocked me. That bubble of perfection I had been living in was slashed open and completely disintegrated, with no conscious way to ever put it back together. While no one is ever fully prepared for death, I now know that, when death comes by suicide, the confusion and anger is another level. Never having experienced real loss or adversity before, and after spending most of my childhood compartmentalizing hard emotions and pushing forward, I couldn't understand the pain Bear must have felt, all alone, sitting on top of his laundry room dryer on the night he pulled the trigger. I couldn't begin to know pain so deep that you would want to die. Or that your hurt trumped your love for your family, friends, and life. I spiraled. And I spiraled fast.

And so began my months'-and years'-long battle with anxiety and depression. I was diagnosed officially with PTSD several weeks after his death. But unofficially, my life had become a hazy dream in which I was barely going through the motions. My body was doing the things I was supposed to be doing—finishing school, going to prom, and attending our graduation ceremony. But me, my soul, hovered above my body, watching from above, as the movie of my final semester of high school played on.

My anxiety became so bad, I had a hard time leaving my mom's side. She slept with me every night for months. Before the days of cell phones and texting, I would just leave school during the day and show up at home, where I would find comfort in her being there. I would slump to the ground, my heart pounding wildly as if it were about to fly out of my chest, and my head racing with all the "what-ifs" that now played on a loop in my mind.

Like, what if I woke up one day and decided to die? What if I was driving my green Cavalier and came to a railroad crossing with a train approaching—would I stop? Or would I drive into it? What if I was on a Ferris wheel and decided to jump out?

My very rational brain knew I didn't want any of those things. But something had changed inside of me, and my chemistry was off. Having no skill to process pain, fear, hurt, and trauma, my mind and all my deepest, darkest fears took over.

For months, I was tormented. For all of my skills at compartmentalizing pain, I couldn't compartmentalize this. There were times when I thought I needed to be locked up in a mental institution, to protect me from hurting myself. I remember being on my bedroom floor, my mom on the phone in the other room, listening as she desperately tried to connect with a psychiatrist to find out what we needed to do.

Soon after that call, Dr. Jan came into my life. And the pills she prescribed were my saving grace. Finally, after months of living in a chronic vagal stress response, the medication allowed me to relax and to begin feeling and processing my pain.

I'll never forget what happened after I took my first Ativan pill. We were sitting down to dinner at my grandparents' house.

For some reason, I was at the head of the table, which was usually reserved for Grandpa. After we said the blessing, when I opened my eyes, I sensed a new feeling wash over me. Calmness moved through my body. It started at my head and flowed to my toes. I could breathe. And in that moment, I remember thinking, *I think I might be okay. I might be able to get through this.* It was the first time I had felt something other than fear or panic since the day of Bear's death.

Our minds have an incredible way of processing trauma, and each of us processes it differently. Even how we process trauma changes over time. That summer of 1998, I knew my mind couldn't process Bear's death alone. My body and mind were exhausted from lack of sleep and the constant state of panic I lived in, and I needed pharmaceutical intervention to begin healing.

I didn't love the idea of taking a pill over more holistic alternatives, and my mom knew this. But she would reassure me, saying things like, "Honey, if you had a heart condition, you would take a pill for it. This is no different. Right now, you have an anxiety condition, and you need to take a pill for it."

And so, I did. That little Ativan pill allowed me the opportunity to quiet my anxiety. To lessen the noise and the irrational thoughts that flowed like Niagara Falls.

It allowed me to enter my freshman year of college; not whole, but not completely broken.

It did another funny little thing. It helped me come to understand that I was depressed. Once the anxiety subsided, it was easy to see. I was sad. I missed Bear. He had been one of my best friends, and he had been hurting. And I hadn't known.

Smells, songs, the fast-food restaurant Pollo Asado, oversized sweatshirts, certain streets in Arvada—they all reminded me of him. And his pain. And now, my pain. I was heartbroken. Heartbroken for him, for his family, for our friends, for mankind.

I went from feeling no pain to feeling the world's pain. I suffered. I cried. A lot. I had relapses of anxiety for years over completely different, but just as irrational, fears. It would take close to seven years before the smell, feel, and sound at the onset of spring didn't trigger me right back into that morning when I learned he had died.

But eventually, I began to heal. While one never truly gets over the loss of a loved one, living with that loss gets easier. And then, life moves forward. I grew, and I learned about pain from the pain.

Chapter 5

Life After Bear

"The sun will rise and set regardless. What you do with its light is up to you."

—Author unknown

INSTEAD OF HEADING to Arizona State University that next fall, as planned, I ended up at Colorado State University. During my senior year of high school, I had only applied to ASU and CSU, because I was so certain I wanted to go to ASU. And I had only applied to CSU as a back-up, because my mom made me.

In May 1998, shortly after Bear died, I had started dating a boy a year older than me who went to CU Boulder, about an hour southwest of Fort Collins, where CSU was located. Once I started college in the fall, I quickly became as codependent on him as I had been on my mom during the months following Bear's death. I was on an emotional roller coaster and leaned on the "stability" of our relationship. He became a crutch, and we spent a lot of time together, despite being in separate towns and at separate schools.

At CSU, I rushed a sorority and made some new girlfriends. But the pull of my boyfriend and Boulder was calling, so I ended up transferring to Boulder for the second semester of my freshman year. Because of my codependency on him, I hadn't realized or understood the emotional control he was exerting over our relationship. We fought a lot, and about things he seemed to have made up. I could never do anything right despite my every best effort.

As much as I worked to accommodate the situation or change my behavior to his liking, the fighting didn't cease, and he continued to pick fights with me. I clung to the fantasy that this person was truly supporting me during the toughest time of my life. I wanted answers but was scared to push too hard, because, ultimately, a fight would occur. Similar to in my childhood, I chose to be easygoing and quick to please, despite what my own feelings and emotions were trying to scream at me. I allowed him to manipulate my mental self-worth, so that I believed I was lucky to be with him. I was full of self-blame and self-doubt.

It wasn't until I finally mustered the courage to break it off with him during my sophomore year that I began to understand the dynamics of our relationship. It wasn't until years later that I understood how people-pleasers and narcissists often come together, using each other to fill their own insecurities and voids; people-pleasers feel fulfilled and valued for their caretaking, and narcissists receive the adoration and praise they crave. At twenty years old, I didn't have the language, tools, or resources to contemplate his behavior and the role I'd played to enable it.

A healthier or more enlightened younger me would have listened to those high-alert warnings and emotions and would have set boundaries. And if those boundaries were crossed, a healthier version of me would have been okay to end the relationship and walk away, despite how scary or vulnerable that would have made me.

Unfortunately, I was none of those things and I looked to others to find my worth and my value. I enjoyed being needed and was eager to please. In turn, this created a barrier around my true self—a barrier that didn't need, want, or ask anything from anyone. I would push forward and work really hard to meet others' needs. The reality was, I didn't know how to be honest about what I was feeling. I actually didn't know I could be honest about how I felt. I just compartmentalized my emotions and moved forward. This barrier "protected me" and "kept me safe."

I realize now that my inability to communicate my feelings or to feel safe about being vulnerable led me to choose relationships with men who were not emotionally available. Perhaps subconsciously, I felt like I was safer with someone who would not force me to be too emotionally vulnerable, and therefore I could continue living a somewhat facile life. In my twenties, really all I wanted was to laugh, have fun, work hard, and give my love to someone who wanted those things, too.

Chapter 6

Fractures

"Change is inevitable. Growth is optional."
—John C. Maxwell

IN EARLY 2006, AT THE AGE of twenty-six, I met my affable and fun, handsome and strong, good-natured and successful soon-to-be husband. We were instantly smitten and things progressed fast. We met in February, and I moved from Denver to Fairfax, Virginia four months later, in June. We were engaged by September and married the following year, in June, 2007. All in all, we'd known each other about sixteen months before we were married. We fell fast, and we fell hard.

The first couple years of our relationship were quite magical. We laughed a lot and played hard. This included many late nights and heavy drinking with friends. We bought a little house in a neighborhood we adored. And we wasted no time getting to work having babies.

But my past experiences predicted my new experience. Josh and I both were emotionally unavailable and did not put time or effort into creating a safe place for either of us to be vulnerable. Because we both were just naturally happy, easygoing people, it didn't seem necessary. It wasn't until much later that I realized we both just stored and compartmentalized hard things. We pushed them away, hoping they would never really resurface. But often they did—mostly when alcohol was involved. Late nights usually resulted in some type of emotional outburst from one of us. And, just as often, between us.

Like many women, I suffered a miscarriage my first pregnancy. The OB/GYN office we first went to handled it horribly. After having the initial ultrasound to listen for the heartbeat, we stood by the nurse's station and waited for the doctor. She came over and, in front of everyone who was standing there, unemotionally told us there was no heartbeat and the baby was not viable. The entire interaction was no more than two minutes long and very sterile. We left in shock.

I didn't tell many people about the miscarriage and, over the next couple of months, was extremely emotional. I was short-tempered and often teary-eyed, and I chalked it up to the hormonal imbalance my body was experiencing. I didn't realize I was mourning. I knew a lot of women who were going through similar situations, and I guess I just didn't feel like I deserved to mourn. I wasn't special or different from anyone else. And so, like much of the other pain I endured over my years, I sucked it up and resumed normal life: being a wife, going to work, and partying with friends.

Fortunately, Josh and I ended up pregnant again fairly quickly and, within twenty months of the initial miscarriage, had two beautiful babies. I felt so blessed. But also, having two babies who were eighteen months apart took a toll on both Josh and me, as well as, ultimately, on our relationship.

UNWINDING PERFECT

I worked very hard to be perfect at everything and to not need help from anyone. Mason, our first child, was a challenging baby and cried almost nonstop. The only help I would accept from anyone was during the hours I worked. The rest of the time, I insisted on doing it all myself. Josh would help where he could, but given Mason's colicky nature, my maternal instinct kicked in, and I took over. Within nine months, I was pregnant again with our second child, Isla, who turned out to be the easiest baby, which was a blessing, because now I was dealing with an eighteen-month-old toddler who had two speeds: on and off.

Something very natural and maternal happens inside women when they have a baby. The only thing that matters for that new mom is her baby and the survival of that baby. My motherly instinct kicked in, and for close to three years, my entire focus was on those two kids and ensuring all of their needs were met.

By the time I looked up to catch my breath, I realized something had shifted drastically in our marriage. My energy and attention, which had once been solely devoted to Josh, were now split between two babies at different ages and stages.

I have distinct memories of being very envious of Josh and what seemed like the carefree lifestyle he still lived. This is not to say he wasn't around, helpful, or a good dad. But he still had late nights with friends and traveled for work, where he got to get away and have sleep-filled nights. I yearned to be able to just disappear for an hour or two without telling anyone and do whatever I wanted, whenever I wanted.

As the years went on and the fissures in our relationship grew, I settled back into the people-pleaser role I knew best. I danced the dance I had learned as a child, making sure not to rock the boat and not to need anything outside the scope of the current arrangement. Things appeared to be okay from the outside. Inside, I was slowly imploding.

By 2013, I knew that our marriage was in big trouble but had no clue how to engage Josh in what would be hard and uncomfortable conversations for both of us. In 2014, I told Josh after one of his late nights that I'd spent hours during the middle of the night separating our household items in my head. Who would get what in a divorce. Surprisingly, he was shocked to hear me say this, but then he hopped on a plane to Dallas, and we never talked about it again. This was how we solved our problems: we simply acted like they did not exist and did not talk about them.

In 2015, we tried couples' therapy for a few sessions. I was not a fan of the therapist, but since Josh seemed to like him, I continued because I was just happy Josh was willing to go. We went together until the session when the therapist told me I wasn't allowed to feel a certain way about one of Josh's behaviors that was my biggest issue in our marriage. He completely invalidated me and left me feeling a little crazy.

After that, I refused to go back. Josh continued on for a couple months more. I remember being nervous to ask Josh if he was still seeing him, maybe because I was worried it would make Josh uncomfortable. Or maybe because I was worried about being uncomfortable with his answer.

About a year later, I finally did ask him if he was still seeing the therapist, and he said he had stopped after he'd realized the man wanted to be more "bros" than in a traditional provider/client relationship. We never sought another therapist, and never learned to communicate. We both just shut down.

So instead of closing the distance, we both let it grow wider and wider, until a massive canyon existed between us. And instead of either of us having the courage to be vulnerable and open, we continued to do the dance we both knew. From the outside, we looked very much like the perfect family. We played the role at school functions, social gatherings, and with our families. From the inside, a heavy, dark cloud hung over us.

Chapter 7

People-Pleasing & Religion

"Taking care of yourself is the most powerful way to begin to take care of others."

—Bryant McGill

BEING A PEOPLE-PLEASER is easier than you think. To never disappoint anyone or let them down, you simply sacrifice what feels right or good to you. You ignore that little voice in your head saying "don't" or "not again." And you certainly don't respond to that physical tightness in your chest or gut reaction that you have when something feels wrong. Hey, if you told someone you would do something, you should do it. You don't want to be flaky, misleading, a liar, or selfish. You want to be easy-going, likable, nice, even lovable...

I worked so hard to be what I thought were those things. But trying to be all things to all people is exhausting and depletes your core self.

Growing up with faithful Christian parents, I was taught to love God, but as a young adult, became scared to death of His "wrath." What I could only imagine were my sinful and shameful behaviors in the eyes of God scared me into routinely inviting

Jesus to come live in my heart, as I was taught, so I would routinely be forgiven. It was a vicious cycle of fear and shame, followed by redemption and fleeting peace. Looking back, it was unhealthy and scary. I wish I had had the ability to comfortably speak about this with a trusted adult, but instead, I battled in my own head. A constant busyness of overthinking, shame, and not being enough flowed through my young mind.

Almost anyone who grew up in a religious setting has grappled with this duality of being a good [name whatever religion you grew up with], and the natural curiosities of being an adolescent. For me, this meant being a good Christian and disciple of Jesus. We went to church almost every Sunday, and as I grew into my teenage years, I went when I wanted to and not because my parents made me. They were lenient and realistic in that way.

My parents never forced religion on my siblings or me and were never religious zealots. They were, however, strong in faith and the teachings of Jesus, which meant they were kind, forgave misgivings, and often slid difficult or unwanted emotions and topics under the rug, so as not to be talked about or processed. We didn't sit around the dinner table and talk about lessons from the Bible or how to merge Sunday school teachings with those of real life. So, I was kind of on my own to interpret and figure out how to be a good Christian, based on what I learned at Sunday school and how I was trying to show up in the world. It was an internal battle between what was authentically me versus what religion said I was supposed to be.

Since childhood, I have always felt a deep connection with God and to a higher spiritual entity. But the lessons I was learning at church often made me feel like I was a bad person. Made me feel guilty. Shameful. Much later in life, when I began my spiritual journey, which led me to unwind many of the patterns and conditioning I learned as a child, I struggled to unite my Christian upbringing with my newfound spirituality. They seemed to conflict with each other: if Jesus was the only one true way to heaven, then how could God be an all-loving God? What about all those people around the world who loved God but didn't believe Jesus was the only savior? Were they condemned to an eternity of hell?

I struggled with this duality and the conflict between what my religion told me and what I felt in my heart. How could only Christians be "saved" in a world where seventy percent of the population weren't Christian? Surely, God would not forsake someone who had never even heard of Jesus.

I couldn't reconcile it in my head. The God I knew instinctively and felt in my everyday spirit, loved everyone. Regardless of race, gender, sexual orientation, and even religion. I felt shameful and guilty for even questioning what I had been taught was truth. But I was also having a hard time connecting with my faith and the dogma of religion. In 2015, I met a very special woman named Tammy. She was the person who ultimately helped me begin to weave together a new understanding of a much bigger and more powerful God than the confines of any single religion. She helped me to realize that religion and spirituality don't have to be in conflict.

As I had been seeking a more authentic connection with God, working with Tammy helped me learn alternative practices to opening my heart and mind that felt truer to me. While religion always felt forced, spirituality felt personal. With spirituality, I could reconcile Jesus's teachings of love and kindness *and* incorporate other ancient philosophies and practices into my daily routines, such as meditation, visualization and pranayama.

As my trust in God returned, so did my ability to become more aware of my behaviors, my choices, my actions, and my inactions. Instead of feeling shameful or guilty about my behavior and sweeping uncomfortable emotions under the rug, I began to address these emotions. I got to know my shadows and began to accept them. Through this, I slowly began the process of healing; building my own set of values, understanding my worth outside of people-pleasing, and creating boundaries.

None of this came fast or easy, and the work was hard. Very luckily, I had support from several healers and spiritual mentors like Tammy over the next several years. They helped me hone awareness of my self-sabotaging behaviors and choices, and in doing so, I eventually was able to mostly break free from them. Stories of these mentors and how they helped me are interspersed throughout the rest of this book, and at the end of the book, there is an Appendix with specific lessons and exercises from some of them.

Chapter 8

Tammy

"Paradise is not a place; it's a state of consciousness."
—Sri Chinmoy

September 18, 2015
Holy f*%$! Tammy!

THIS WAS THE FIRST THING I wrote in my journal after seeing Tammy for our initial session. While Tammy was a healer and a life coach, there was something about her that was different from any other coach I had met before. It was like she stared deeply into my soul and saw every fear, insecurity, hope, and dream I had ever had. Then, through her work, she slowly began to help me unwind my fears and insecurities, while strengthening my conviction toward my hopes and dreams.

I don't know if words can describe Tammy's unique magnetism. Her entire way of being was kind and gentle, yet formidable and strong. Energetically, her smile could shift a room, and her wisdom came from a deep connection to the spiritual world. She had the knowledge and understanding of many master gurus and the beauty and grace of a movie star. Before becoming a life coach and healer, she was a businesswoman who had owned and operated a very popular Denver restaurant. She worked the front of the house like no other and made sure the operations in the back ran smoothly.

When I first met Tammy, I had just made a major career transition from being a medical device sales representative to joining a friend who was building a healthcare technology company he had founded called Matrix Analytics (which we rebranded to Eon a couple years later). My friend, who later became my business partner, asked me to be the first CEO of his company, and I had politely declined. In my mind, I was "only" a sales rep, and what did I know about running a company? When I did end up joining the company, several months later, it was as a VP, and I reported directly to the new CEO.

I was insecure about this job title, and although, intrinsically, I knew everything that I needed to do to be successful, I didn't trust myself. I assumed the CEO knew much more than I did and found myself doing a familiar dance of dimming my light so as not to overshadow him or other employees who I assumed knew start-up life much better than I did. I did all of this without even knowing I was doing it.

I talked about my insecurities with Tammy and how I would respond to my new coworkers. She taught me about the power of the subconscious mind and how it runs about ninety-five percent of our daily lives. This meant I was only consciously living five percent of the time! Bad habits, fears, and anxiety lie deep within the subconscious mind, conditioned from a young age, and eagerly pop out to "protect us" without our even knowing it.

To help me begin to combat my insecurities and auto-responses, she taught me to tap positive affirmations into my heart center. Tapping, or Emotional Freedom Technique (EFT), is a self-help therapy technique based in traditional Chinese medicine. It connects the mind to the body to help rewire certain subconscious ways of thinking. Tapping acupoints on the body while simultaneously verbally expressing positive affirmations, called Self-Affirmation Theory, is another self-help therapy technique. By combining these techniques, you can begin to dismantle negative thought patterns and build new neural pathways that carry fresh ways of thinking about yourself.

Repeating positive affirmations and simultaneously tapping challenges and disrupts negative thought cycles and patterns, and can begin to reprogram the negative patterning that one has created over time. Studies have even shown under magnetic resonance imaging (MRI) that self-affirmation increases these new neural pathways. Specifically, the ventromedial prefrontal cortex becomes more active, which is the part of the brain responsible for positive valuation and self-related information processing (Falk et al., 2015; Cascio et al., 2016).

Tammy suggested the first two positive affirmations for me to "tap-in" were, "I love myself unconditionally," and "I trust myself." Each day, while tapping on my chest, I would say, "I love myself unconditionally," "I love myself unconditionally," "I love myself unconditionally." And then, "I trust myself," "I trust myself," "I trust myself."

I quickly learned I had no idea what it meant to love myself unconditionally. And I certainly didn't trust myself or my decisions. I was self-critical, and I second-guessed everything I did—my decisions, my conversations, etc. I was so worried about not disappointing anyone and ensuring I showed up as I thought they wanted to see me, I never really knew if any of what I was doing was right.

And then, I realized, if I couldn't love myself unconditionally or trust myself to ask for my needs to be met, how was anyone else going to ever truly love me or meet my needs?

This was a profound realization and set the wheels in motion for much of the self-discovery and internal work that lay ahead for me. I barely understood the power of the subconscious mind or how the tapping worked, but I was laying the groundwork to rewire self-critical negative feedback loops I had spent most of my life creating.

My time with Tammy and the practices she helped me develop left me feeling more secure about my innate abilities and less critical about my everyday actions. For better or worse, it opened a Pandora's Box, and so began what would become my lifelong journey to heal the trauma and core wounds from my childhood, and begin the quest to seek the truth about my life's purpose.

My first step was to develop a gradual awareness of the emotions I had been compartmentalizing much of my life; mainly my insecurities and feelings of shame, inadequacy, and self-doubt.

During childhood, whenever something hurt my feelings or bothered me, my very well-intentioned mom placated the situation by finding the rationale behind the other person's actions. It was very empathetic to the other person's situation but left little room for validation of my feelings.

Over the years, I realized both my sister and I had picked up this same trait. Someone would share a problem with one of us, and immediately, we would try to explain why the other person had done what they did. It wasn't until I started to become aware of my feelings and the fact that they were valid that I began to understand the system put in place around emotions during my childhood. Sometimes, all you need is for someone to say, "Yeah, that really stinks. I'm sorry that happened."

I had allowed my feelings to be invalidated most of my life, mainly because I didn't know what healthy validation looked like.

From that same initial journal entry about Tammy on September 18, 2015, I wrote:

> *Tammy told me today that, when it comes to emotions, remember to set boundaries with others who don't respect your emotions or refuse to validate them, and put systems in place to control them [our emotions]. Over and over, we allow ourselves to be victimized, and therefore we're not allowed to feel our own emotions. When we realize that our emotions are valid, we are set free.*

While it would take years for me to truly understand how to live by Tammy's words, she offered new insight into a blind spot of mine. I was allowing myself to be victimized by not creating healthy boundaries for myself. My unease and inability to stand up for my own needs essentially created a vicious cycle where I hoped others would show up for me how I needed them to, and then would be grossly disappointed when they didn't.

By beginning to allow myself to feel some of my own emotions, I became stronger. I started to realize there was power in my emotions—by honoring them, and also by simply recognizing them. Things that had hurt me before began to not hurt me as much. Doors began to open, and new paths were revealed.

I saw Tammy regularly for the next year—mostly when I started to feel a tightness in my chest or anxiety about something not in my control. But as often happens in life, as things got busier and busier at home and work, many of the practices I had learned from Tammy faded. I got wrapped up in life and began what I can only describe as a downward spiral.

Chapter 9

Life Happens

"In three words I can sum up everything I've learned about life; it goes on."

—Robert Frost

OVER THE NEXT COUPLE of years, I saw Tammy only a few times. I was shifting my daily focus and energy as my partners and I began to build the new business, and I was running a household. In March 2016, we sold our house to build a new home, moving into a lovely rental that was outside of our neighborhood, so the commute back and forth for school and activities was exhausting. I also was responsible for most of the decisions at the building project, so essentially was doing three jobs at once.

I was managing all the changes at home, and the new business was flourishing. I spent every waking moment fully dedicated to Eon, to my children (who often took a backseat to my ambitions with the business), to completing the new house, and commuting. During this time, some pretty significant events occurred between Josh and me, which led to an even greater fissure between us and left me little hope we'd find a path back to each other. While deep in my heart I knew I was unhappy, I thought my role was to continue on being the "good girl" I had learned to be at such a young age.

The life I was living was exhausting and not sustainable. I didn't know it at the time, but, essentially, I had gone into survival mode and let my yang (masculine) energy lead. This allowed me to hold everything together and accomplish a crazy amount of work every day. But it also meant I was direct, often short, and conquered each day as if I were a warrior in battle. I deviated from my yin (feminine) energy, which had given me space to write and meditate and helped me connect deeply with friends. My heart-centric practice of self-love and gratitude became a fading memory.

And then, my hair started to fall out. Literally. Every time I washed my hair, what looked like a small mouse would end up in my drain. It became so bad, I basically was left with a mullet. I was stressed beyond my max, unhealthy, and exhausted.

I finally reached back out to Tammy in early 2018 and was joyful to see her. We caught up. I told her about my ambitions, the business's accomplishments, and my daily stress. She told me it was okay that I had been gone for a couple years, that it had actually been necessary for me to accomplish what I needed to accomplish in the business during that time. This was the first time I pieced together how the yin and the yang of energy—the feminine and the masculine—could actually play a role within my own being.

According to ancient Chinese medicine, all things have both yin and yang qualities that seek to find balance between them. While they represent polarity, they also are interdependent—one cannot exist without the other. Yin represents nurture, intuition, relaxation, and imagination. Yang represents enthusiasm, directness, production, and activity. I had inadvertently become so productive by the "doing" of all three of my obligations that I had little time to relax, daydream, or nurture my inner being. My health was suffering because I had completely turned off access to the yin within me. Tammy and I spent many hours discussing this.

And then, she dropped a major bomb. She told me her cancer, which she had fought off four years before, had returned. At that moment, I knew Tammy was going to die. I don't know why I knew it or how I knew it. But I knew it would be one of the last times I saw her.

As it turned it, it *was* the last time I saw her. I reached out several times over the next year, but her cancer made her too weak to see anyone. She passed away on August 9, 2019.

I had spent so much of the previous years "thriving" in my masculine energy that I had disconnected from my heart. I had completely stepped away from Tammy, my meditation, journaling, and any other yin activity that had kept me grounded and centered. Tammy was an important teacher and the beginning of my spiritual journey. I was heartbroken that I never got to say goodbye.

While stepping into my masculine energy had been necessary for me to accomplish what I needed to accomplish with the business, my family, and our new home, I wish I had spent more time with Tammy. I can still close my eyes and see her generous smile, feel her gentle ease, and hear her warm laugh. She was a warrior yet kind and at ease.

Chapter 10

Imposter Syndrome

"And it's fine to fake it 'til you make it. 'Til you do. 'Til it's true."

—Taylor Swift, *Snow on the Beach*

IN 2015, I HAD STRUGGLED inwardly when I transitioned from being a sales rep in a large corporate setting to being the VP of Business Development for Eon, a healthcare technology start-up. It wasn't because the work was harder or that I wasn't competent. I struggled because I didn't feel like I had earned the right to jump titles from a sales rep to vice president.

Working for global companies like Stryker, Baxter and Medtronic, my career trajectory had already been decided for me. Be a top sales rep, be likable by upper management, contribute cross departmentally, and then climb a massive corporate ladder, but only as long as upper management stacks and ranks you high enough. The companies I had worked for had enormous budgets, layers of management, and billions of dollars in revenue.

Like any good imposter, I felt ashamed that, suddenly, I had a big fancy title that seemed unearned. I was embarrassed to say *VP* to former colleagues and peers, worried they would wonder who in the heck I thought I was, when, weeks ago, we'd held the same title. I was now Vice President of Business Development, and only because I had turned down the offer to be the first CEO, when my former business partner and founder of the company initially asked me. My response to him when he had asked was, "I'm a sales rep. What do I know about running a business?"

Turns out, I knew quite a lot, but it would take me many years for my self-confidence to match my competence. By August 2016, I had been promoted to president of the business, and eventually, to co-CEO in 2018.

Corporate America is structurally built on layers of management. You have entry level, manager, mid-level, another manager, maybe next a district or regional or national manager, then a VP, a president, and, finally, the executive layer. Most employees have some goal to work their way up from entry-level roles and salaries into something with more responsibility. In addition to the sheer size of large corporations, oftentimes, being promoted is more about who you know versus what you know.

Right before I joined Eon, I had interviewed for the Regional Manager position of my region at Medtronic. I had been a top sales rep for my entire sales career and was Rep of the Year my first year at Medtronic. The manager who hired me was leaving, and they were looking for an internal replacement. The team liked me. I had always been a natural leader, with management experience, and I thought I was a shoo-in.

As it turned out, the VP of our division had just left as well, and a new VP had come in. He was ultimately the decision maker for the management position, and instead of promoting internally, he hired a guy he knew from previous companies.

Nepotism, inflated egos, and over-exaggerated résumés are rampant in corporate America, and making significant career jumps can be stagnated when you are not part of that inner group.

That's not to say there isn't nepotism in the start-up world, but at least there, you can't hide. You're fully exposed, all day, every day. In large corporations, where layers are thick and budgets are deep, employees can hide. They can be low performers, fly under the radar, and still get promoted. Even at the VP level and above.

I was ignorant to this at the time. I thought, if you were a VP, you were something special and had worked hard to get there. Not to say there are not plenty of great VPs out there who have earned every bit of their position. But a title, as it turns out, is more of a mindset than anything else.

So, when I joined Eon as a VP, self-doubting questions cycled through my head on repeat. What did I know about running a business unit? I asked myself this even though I had been running my own business unit successfully since I started my career. Even though my dad was a successful entrepreneur from whom I had learned a lot, and I asked myself this despite the fact that I had been hustling small entrepreneurial endeavors for almost two decades by that time. I felt like a total imposter. A title of VP? How could one go from sales rep to VP and be taken seriously? Wouldn't all my peers at Medtronic see through me as only a sales rep?

I was also intimidated by the first CEO, who had been hired when I declined. I thought he knew more about building a business than I did and was better equipped to run the business. He was a smooth talker, and it just seemed like he had it all figured out. He always had an answer that rolled right off his tongue, even if there was no actual substance behind it.

Add to my intimidation the pressure to perform in front of VCs and PE companies. At the time, we didn't have a concise value statement or explanation of what we did, and smooth talking is *not* something I'm good at if I'm caught off guard or don't know the answer. Basically, I'm awful at bullshitting.

When I would cold-call investment companies and deliver the "elevator pitch," I would freeze when questions started being asked about market opportunity, company valuation, the type of money we were raising, how we integrated into EHRs, etc. These were all questions I would make sure I was able to answer for the next time I was asked, but when thrown off, I could hardly string three coherent sentences together, because I would get so nervous.

To this day, I still get so embarrassed, thinking about the first in-person fundraising pitch I made. We were no-name, first-time entrepreneurs starting a company most people did not understand. Our friends and family network became our lifeline for fundraising.

I reached out to a friendly acquaintance, who, at the time, was a portfolio manager at Marsico Capital Management, a local Denver-based investment management firm. He was kind enough to take a meeting with us. I was so excited—I wanted very badly to make an early impact and help get this company off the ground. This was toward the end of 2015 and the very beginning of my career with Eon.

The day before our meeting, I put together a pitch deck and practiced in my head what I was going to say. At dinner that night, I showed the deck to Josh, and tried to articulate to him what I was planning to pitch. I struggled with it, and I could see in his face he was trying to be supportive but was becoming a bit worried. I remember telling him, and trying to convince myself, I'd be okay. I was, after all, used to speaking in front of large groups of doctors and clinicians about what it was I was selling, so how could pitching to a friendly investment opportunity be any harder?

Turns out, for me, it was.

The founder of Eon, the CEO, and I all showed up to the Marsico office downtown. It was on the seventeenth floor of a beautiful high-rise, where my friend was waiting for us. We went into his office, and, after a little small talk, I opened my computer and the deck. And I tried to talk.

I tried to explain how we were creating a technology that would prevent thousands, maybe millions, of people from slipping through the cracks of healthcare and potentially save just as many lives. I wanted to tell him we were a small team, but the right team to accomplish all of this. And that we were seeking a small amount of seed capital, so we could improve our minimally viable product (MVP) and deploy it at a beta hospital site.

But instead of saying all of that, I froze. Words wouldn't come –not in coherent sentences or even out at all. I looked at my coworkers and could see panic in their eyes. My brain had completely quit me, and I was paralyzed.

Fortunately, the company founder stepped in and was able to eloquently articulate everything I had tried to say. I don't know if I have ever been so embarrassed. First, to ask a friend for a favor and then to completely bomb, but second, to perform so badly in front of the two people who had just hired me to fundraise and sell. While both were gracious and kind to me after, the experience left an embedded somatic response to pitching that would continue to be triggered for quite some time after.

In any meeting after that, either virtual or in-person, my fight-or-flight would kick in. My heart would start to pound, my stomach would flip-flop, and as soon as I began to speak, my voice would get so shaky and breathy, it was like I had just run a marathon. Once I had been talking long enough and able to get out of my head, my physical nerves would calm down, and I would be fine. But the shaky voice would become the bane of my presenting existence for many years.

Our egos have a funny way of trying to protect us—in my case, my ego was sending high-alert warnings to try to get me to avoid presenting so my ego would never again have to suffer from the same embarrassment I had felt that day, presenting to my friend. Our ego and subconscious minds are programmed to "protect" us—sometimes from real threats, but often from unprocessed traumas that can be triggered by similar-feeling scenarios.

In my mind, however, at the time, it just proved I was an imposter and hadn't earned the right to that vice president title. A true VP wouldn't clam up when giving a presentation, and the shaky voice was a sign of failure and weakness. How could anyone take me seriously? How could I take myself seriously?

The internal battle waged. But externally, I kept showing up. I kept making calls. I kept putting myself out there. The founder and I got into a rhythm, and before long, we had signed our first two clients. The first was a small critical-access hospital on the western slope of Colorado. The second, a massive academic healthcare institution in the Midwest. Before we knew it, we were legitimate. And so was I. Internally, I knew it, too.

It quickly became obvious I was doing the role that the CEO should be doing, and so, when he left in August 2016, I became President of the company. This time, I knew I had earned it, and I was ready to step into my role. Fully.

At Eon, we did a lot with a little. That meant each of us did the work of two or three full-time employees for many years. I personally felt I had to do extra—to go above and beyond to prove my worth, my loyalty, my value—each and every day. I never wanted anyone to question if I deserved my title and role. By 2018, we had emerged as the market leader, servicing several major U.S. healthcare systems, and it was obvious our dynamic partnership was working.

The saying, "fake it until you make it," couldn't have been more true. Whether it was how I felt when I first became a VP, or how we wanted the company to be perceived externally, a healthy dose of faking it until you make it goes a long way. We hustled hard, and it was important to appear as big and bold as we knew we would become.

Chapter 11

Authenticity

"A mind that is stretched by a new experience can never go back to its old dimensions."

—Oliver Wendell Holmes, Jr.

TWO MAJOR EVENTS happened in May 2018. First, we rebranded the company from its original name to Eon, and I became co-CEO. Second, I was asked to give a commencement speech at the University of Colorado, my alma mater, for the political science department, where I did my degree minor.

The imposter syndrome I was experiencing made both things feel wrong to me. Even though I had been operating the business since 2016, I couldn't allow myself to think I was a CEO. Me? A Chief Executive Officer?

There was a "co" in front of it, which meant I had a partner and ultimately wasn't the sole CEO, but for whatever reason, I could not allow myself to feel comfortable with this title. I remember thinking I was a fraud. I didn't get an MBA. I didn't even have a business degree. I was just a gal who'd hustled my whole life to do the best I could at everything I did, because failure was never an option. Now, as co-CEO, I might fail. I might be exposed as someone who just hustled. Maybe I wasn't good enough or smart enough.

At the same time, the fear within me wanted to turn down the commencement speech offer, but I knew I would regret it if I did. I was terrified, not so much that I couldn't write a great speech, but that I couldn't deliver it. A wide range of emotions coursed through my veins, but most of all, I couldn't believe a higher-learning institution thought I was good enough to give a commencement speech. Reconciling how people viewed me externally with how I saw myself internally was difficult. But I knew in my bones it was something I was supposed to do. So, I worked for weeks to write the perfect speech and then practiced for countless hours.

Given my incessant need always to present as perfect, and my uneasiness with being vulnerable, I didn't want any of my family there. The thought of crashing and burning in front of them was a hundred-times scarier than totally whiffing it in front of a thousand strangers. I felt exposed and vulnerable–both things I was not comfortable sharing with my family.

The hours spent practicing paid off, and the speech was great. I had purposefully added a quick blurb at the beginning of my speech that addressed my shaky voice–I figured it was better for me to call attention to it and recognize it for what it was versus not. Somehow, by honoring it, I was able to accept it, and it quickly dissipated. While I still couldn't believe the University of Colorado had thought me worthy to give a commencement speech, it did build my confidence and help me to become less nervous about speaking publicly, going forward,

What I didn't know, believe, or understand at the time was that I was just as good as, and oftentimes better than, many of the executives we were working with. Over time, I started to see that everyone had their own unique skills and talents, and once I was able to harness mine, I was more than acceptable as a co-CEO. The other co-CEO was the founder of Eon, and together, we complemented each other beautifully. You know what else we did? We kicked ass. We grew the business. We grew ourselves. And we made an excellent team.

By early 2021, after Covid had settled a bit, I began to really feel in every part of me that I was a co-CEO. I started trusting my decisions. I knew my value. And I felt like I was home. I *loved* building our team. And I loved being a leader for them. I cherished mentoring and engaging with employees. I *loved* our clients, solving their institutional challenges and making them happy. I *loved* our mission and what we stood for—that we didn't just talk about it, but we *were* about it. We were on a mission to make patients healthier and healthcare affordable. And we were doing that.

After I returned from a personal trip to France in 2022, I presented to the entire company at a monthly townhall. I usually ran these meetings and typically would talk about the current state of the business. But at this meeting, I decided to talk about lessons I had learned cycling through France and how they applied to business.

I created a PowerPoint that included photos I had taken from the trip, and I shared photos such as a slug in the middle of the road, with silly titles like, "Don't be a slug." Or a picture of a gorgeous poppy field that had popped up out of nowhere around a bend, and the title, "You never know what is around the corner." Or the most embarrassing one, where I was in full cyclist gear (I had never ridden a road bike more than fifteen miles at one time before this trip): cyclist sunglasses, helmet, and pursed lips. Like I'm a real cyclist somebody. And the title, "You are not an imposter." It was a fun meeting, and I felt relaxed and at ease.

But the most special thing that came out of that meeting was how the team responded. I received so many emails and direct messages from different team members about how well they liked the meeting and how authentic it had felt. They liked that I had threaded real life into the business message. And appreciated how I had been vulnerable with them about some of my fears and insecurities about the trip.

It was only then that I realized people wanted to hear what I had to say. I had spent my entire life blending into larger groups of people, so uncomfortable with all eyes on me, keeping my answers to questions short and trying to ask more questions than I was asked. I had never wanted to take up too much of anyone's time, and I certainly didn't think what I had to say was interesting enough to capture an audience.

Now, I was learning, people wanted to hear what I had to say. And I felt compelled to share more. To go deeper. To be more authentic. So, as my time as co-CEO continued, I slowly became more comfortable with authentic storytelling. I stopped worrying about being so scripted and allowed myself to just flow.

* * *

I want to take this moment to thank all of you amazing Eon employees who took the time to reach out to me at some point over the years, to tell me you liked or appreciated my messages.

Thank you.

I want you to know how much those notes, emails, and DMs meant to me. They are forever in my heart, and they have encouraged me to continue to share my story. Quite frankly, I don't think I would have ever had the courage to publish this book without those messages. I am forever grateful to each of you and the impact you have had on me.

* * *

The years it took for me to get to the point where I felt I deserved a title or trusted myself were not easy. I doubted my actions and decisions over and over, and I had so much fear that people would not see me as an equal. Some of it was real, but much of it was my own limiting fear. I learned that I couldn't control what someone thought of me. Even when I was mistaken as the secretary or admin in virtual meetings, because I was the only female on the call (yes, this still happens), eventually, instead of getting hurt or mad, I began to laugh about it and just brush it off.

Because, at the end of the day, who cares? I know who I am, I know my value, and I know what I have to offer.

But—that imposter syndrome is real, and when you are going through it, even minute little interactions can reinforce the negative self-talk in one's head.

The early co-CEO in me just put my head down, was a task-monster, and became wholly and fully committed to overseeing (which, I later realized, meant *controlling*) just about every task and function that fell under my purview. I had to see, touch, know, write, interact with, or be a part of every meeting, marketing material, financial decision, personnel hire, customer, etc. (This continued even after I worked through my imposter syndrome.)

But those early days were different. I overcommitted much of the time. I was tactical, I was methodical, I was overly dependable. I did a lot of work. I made sure no balls ever dropped and that the train stayed on the tracks. I made sure no one was ever disappointed and that I was all things to all people.

I did all of that until two things began to happen: I started getting sick. Like really, really sick. And I started to realize that the facade I wore, and my compulsive need to please, actually were not pleasing anyone and were in fact disappointing just about everyone. I was unintentionally hurting and disappointing people I loved and cared about the most.

Chapter 12

The Start of an Awakening

"True happiness is… to enjoy the present, without anxious dependence upon the future."

—Lucius Annaeus Seneca

I TURNED FORTY IN November 2019. While I was mostly okay with the milestone, I did encounter several mini-midlife crises building up to my fortieth birthday. When I was at work, I was feeling guilty about my kids. If I was with my kids, I was feeling guilty about the business. An inner battle was waging war, and an inescapable duality lived within me.

I wrote in October of 2019:

> *Is it weird to freak out about 40 one minute and then feel totally at ease another? I go through mini-midlife crises regularly. I want to work hard and have tons of beneficial influence to mankind. Then, the next minute, I want to quit my job and have more babies and be a stay-at-home mom. Then, my brain battles that I want to keep my job but back off. Next, I want to quit. And then, five seconds later, I'm back to loving my job and wanting to work my ass off.*

UNWINDING PERFECT

The noise in my head at the end of 2019 was at an all-time high, and I was running on fumes. I loved my job, solving complex problems, and building our amazing business. I loved work: the joy and fulfillment it brought me, my independence and the self-worth I felt, and our growing team. But, on the other hand, I was missing out on major moments in my kids' childhood. I missed more Valentine and Halloween parties than I care to admit, and I yearned to be closer to them and more present with them. I was torn between two worlds and had no idea how to reconcile them. So, I just did what I was good at—I compartmentalized everything, including my feelings, and I prioritized others' needs over mine, including my health. I just continued to push... No, to sprint through life.

By the end of 2019, something had to give. I was literally working myself to death. I was a very poor version of myself, emotionally, physically, and spiritually. And by not taking care of me, I was not able to take care of anyone else. I started getting sick more regularly, and I was cranky! As a generally happy and optimistic person, feeling irritable and out of sorts was an uncomfortable place for me to reside.

> *January 2, 2020*
>
> *I've had such a hard time these last eight weeks. Too much travel between Josh and me, too crazy with the holidays. Work... crazy, big, upending events. So many changes, but so much opportunity. I was soooo tired. And unhappy. Friday after Christmas, I got 11 hours of sleep and was a new person! Yea! Then almost immediately got cranky again.*

I've been cranky a lot lately, I've realized. Not happy. Pulled in so many directions.

   Work. Travel. Kids. Home. Lack of sleep.

      Woe is me. Boo!

I have the opportunity of a lifetime.

   I'm so tired.

Get some sleep!!!! You are not a machine

   I feel disconnected from my kids.

Connect! Be present

   I'm too busy.

Then plan better. Say "no" to things.

I knew I was overextending myself, and one side of my brain was crying out for help. And then, the rational, practical side would offer a solution. But despite my best efforts, I was never able to follow my own advice, and I continued the tailspin.

With Tammy's passing, I had lost a tool in my toolbelt, the one that helped me manage my life stresses, including my negative inner critic, my fears, and my unhealthy addiction to work (which, in reality, was just a void-filler, because so much was lacking in my personal life that I clung to work to fill those voids).

Although Tammy could never be replaced, a new network of healers, whom I affectionately started referring to as my gurus, began to enter my life. My "gurus" were really a mix of coaches and mentors who ultimately played some role in my unwinding of perfect. Each would play a significant part in my quest for self-discovery I unknowingly was about to embark on. The first was Zoe Rodriguez.

I met Zoe in January 2020. She had been a close friend of Tammy's, and they often practiced together. Zoe specialized (and still does) in massage therapy and Reiki and is a gifted medium.

I remember lying on Zoe's massage table that first session and having the same moment of relief as I had had so many years before, after Bear's passing, when I finally felt a sense of calming through my head and body. I remember thinking, "Wow. I'm going to be okay."

During our session, and through Zoe's gift of clairvoyance, she confirmed many things that I already knew deep within me. This included how I was running on adrenaline and fumes. That I overcomplicate things by overanalyzing and make them much harder than they need to be. That I needed to be more mindful and consciously create, instead of going through everyday motions unconsciously and without being present. And that I needed to get back to the practice Tammy had taught me about EFT and Self-Affirmation Theory. This time, I needed to tap, "I welcome ease and grace into my life."

Zoe also shared things with me that I might have known but didn't want to hear and therefore ignored. This included that I needed to let go of control and delegate more, and that I was often too focused on the wrong things. She knew I needed to hire additional people to do the busy work I was doing and needed to find space. Needed to "soften my edges." (I remember thinking, "How can I soften my edges? I'm in a constant battle in all things in my life. Kill or be killed. Eat or be eaten.")

And then, she told me things I didn't know and were a surprise to me. She said I had a lot of creative energy and needed to use it. She said I was a creative thinker with good ideas, and I needed to do more creative writing. Ironically, she was the first of four different people who would tell me, over the next couple of years, that I needed to write more.

She told me I needed to meditate for twenty minutes every day, that it would allow me space to increase my mindfulness and allow me to operate at a higher level.

I left that first session with Zoe with renewed hope. She had shifted much of the negative and heavy energy that was stuck inside of me and had shared messages with me that I needed to hear, many of which were a good kick in the rear. She reminded me that I was the controller of my own destiny— of both the good and the bad I had created. It was up to me to take control of the things I didn't like and wanted changed.

I was so ready to get back to me. I wrote in my journal about Zoe later that night.

January 3, 2020

I really want to get back to myself. Joyful. Happy. Playful. Present. ENGAGED! When have I been engaged? I've been so distracted for so long. Time to be present. With intentions. 2020 is my year.

Chapter 13

A Transformative Catalyst

"Wellness is a connection of paths: knowledge and action."
—Joshua Holtz

I'M PRETTY SURE I HAD COVID before Covid was a thing. Besides running myself down and getting very sick the end of 2019, I was incredibly sick for almost ten days at the end of January 2020. My kids were both sick, and so was my husband.

Josh took NyQuil for three days straight and slept, felt great after that, and hopped on a flight to Scotland for work. I was left to take care of our kids, who were both equally sick but had nuances in their symptoms. Since we had tested negative for flu and strep, our doctors chalked it up to a cold and told us to rest.

Mason, our son, was sick first and had a bad cough, sore throat, and headache. He was fine about three days later but, similar to viral reactions he had had before, he woke up on the fourth morning and could not walk. His lower legs became so weak and his calf muscles so tight, he literally had to crawl on the floor, because it was so painful to walk. This is an uncommon side effect of viral infections, but when it does occur, it's usually in boys and is called benign childhood myositis.

Isla, our daughter, experienced extreme croup for about a week and had to have several steroid treatments from the doctor. She would wake up in the middle of the night, unable to breathe, and panicked. We would make a steamy shower, and she would hop in. In some of the severe instances, we threw open the doors to outside and let the cold air rush into her lungs. It was scary.

And for me, I was just beyond sick. I had a high fever for several days, shortness of breath, extreme fatigue, and general malaise. I can't take NyQuil, because it has the opposite effect on me, and I become anxious and wired. I was coughing so much, I couldn't sleep at night, my body rife with spasms and unable to relax enough to allow sleep to enter. I was exhausted.

For whatever reason, I took a virtual meeting with one of our largest clients in the middle of being so sick. I sounded awful and had no business being on the call. In hindsight, I should have asked someone to cover for me. But at that time, my mentality was never to disappoint anyone or put anyone out, even if it meant putting myself out. I would go to great extremes to "please" others, as this was how I thought I showed my value. I was always on and always available.

Once I finally recovered from the mystery virus, my energy was never quite the same. Around 3 p.m. every day, I would crash, and I would get an odd sore throat and a headache. It happened like clockwork. Because my self-value was so closely tied to my productivity, I didn't know how to recognize that my body needed a break and that I should rest. As I fought through the fatigue, I found myself barely able to concentrate or produce adequate work during the last couple hours of the day. I was, in fact, doing the opposite of what I was trying to achieve by not resting.

After several doctor's visits that yielded few answers, I decided to reach out to a medical intuitive with whom a couple of my friends had very positive experiences. I met Davie Blu Fuller in March 2020, right before the world shut down. I'm not exaggerating when I say Davie helped me change my life.

What Davie shared with me that first day initiated a journey into my shadows that until then, I had been completely unaware of. Topics such as core wounds and subsequent coping behaviors dominated the conversation. These revelations catalyzed deep introspection; the need to unpack years of compartmentalizing, to face truths that I had long since buried, and later, resulting in resolution of fears. This transformative journey unfolded over the next couple of years and forever changed me. Something deep within me knew the person that I was becoming had always been there, but had felt silenced and afraid to shine, never worthy of being shown to the world. Once I made the conscious decision to do the work to begin to heal core wounds, the truest version of me started to emerge.

Chapter 14

Davie Blu

"Sometimes, the messages we receive are not what we want to hear, but they are always what we need to hear."

—Davie Blu Fuller

DAVIE AND I MET for the first time on March 14, 2020. She knew nothing about me yet somehow knew everything about me. What I learned that first session was that Davie had the ability to remove life's noise and focus on what was important. She was able to thread my conscious and subconscious into a knowing that I did not yet quite understand. She spoke to both my soul and my heart and saw me as the perfectly and uniquely flawed human being that I am. She understood the "why" behind my motivators and brought light to my core wounds. And did all of this with love and without judgment.

Before any meeting, Davie does what is called an "invocation of the soul." She energetically asks the client's higher self for permission to tap into their higher being and then receives messages that she describes as "in divine timing;" meaning the exact right messages that each client needs to hear at that exact moment.

UNWINDING PERFECT

When Davie performs an invocation on her clients, she receives divine messages and writes them down. Then, when she meets with her client, she shares each message through a thoughtful and engaging conversation.

Below are her notes from my first invocation and our first session. The regular font are the messages from her invocation, and the italicized print are the notes she took from our discussion.

Invocation 3/14/20

Allow yourself to receive, to balance your Yin and Yang energy. I became emotional when I tapped into this. *I felt so emotional when I tapped in and wanted to cry but would not allow myself to cry or to feel the emotions. I pushed them aside to carry on—get on with my day. Remember that, when our fight-or-flight is stuck in one position and we are in fear mode, we may be operating from our Yang energy. When we allow ourselves to heal, we can bring in more of our feminine energy or the Yin.*

Try to balance the two of these, so you don't feel like you have the world on your shoulders every day. Also, try to allow yourself to receive—to really receive. You don't always have to be the giver or the caretaker. You don't always need to take control and do, do, do. Read your cards, and let those sink in—they speak a lot about this.

Control core wound. *This seems to be your most prevalent core wound. This wound also triggers all your other core wounds.*

Allow yourself to truly surrender to the changes you want to implement. You are holding on. Let go. You are not wrong. *You* want to make changes but, at times, don't. This can be due to lack of trust or, when you go to make changes, your control core wound gets in the way to remind you as to why you should not make changes. That it may not be "safe." That you can't control the outcome, so why make risky and uncalculated changes.

So, in order to make changes for your highest good, you may want to try to heal some wounds, so you can make the decisions from a place of clear sight and not fear or panic. They also say that you are not wrong with what you want to change—sit with this one.

Life balance—allow yourself to find this. To implement this.

Need to control the outcome. Going into the future to problem-solve and to worry.

Let your authentic self make decisions. Don't make them from your need to control.

Inflammation. EBV—Epstein Barr Virus. Maybe dormant at times, but stress will activate it. Heavy metals. Do a detox.

You want to let go, but your core wound of control brings you back to where you started. *Remember, we spoke a lot about the either/or. There are so many choices and options in the middle. There doesn't have to be just an either.*

Why do you want what you want? How did you get here? Who really made the decisions? *Sit with this one. Write it down and try to unravel. Can you find the source of your motivations? To your fear and worry? For your need for control?*

Let emotions out. It's great that you allow yourself to have a good cry every now and then. I'm sure it's a wonderful release. But try to see what the emotions are when you don't allow yourself to cry. *What emotions are you suppressing or avoiding? What triggers these emotions? Try to track this.*

Try a list regarding worries. List what is relevant now and what is a future worry. Is there anything you can tick off the list and let go of, mentally and energetically?

Wear many hats. Obligation.

Deconstruct your labels. This carries the potential for big change. *I sent you homework on how to start this.*

Imbalance with home life. *We elaborated on this in great detail.*

Emotional.

Kept wanting to release emotion and cry but would stop myself.

Control and peace cannot co-exist—ever. *This is huge.*

Are your fears real or perceived? Process this moment to moment. *Real is happening right now. Perceived is when it's not happening but may or may not. Try to use this one to see what you are really worrying about. Are they real fears that need your attention, or future? There is a Divine order to things. Are you using your energy for things that may or may not happen? Are you worrying out of order, with putting the cart before the horse?*

Control and predictability make you feel safe. Because of this, you struggle to let go of what no longer serves you. Even when you want change. *Sometimes we stay in unwanted patterns because they do give us predictability, and sometimes, people can fear the unknown. You can't look before you leap sometimes. You cannot map out the future, see it, and then start walking toward it. Doesn't work that way.*

Unravel the root cause of your control wound to liberate yourself. You may not move forward until you do.

You have an advanced awareness but stay stuck. Core wound work. *You are well-educated about a lot. BUT working on the core wounds will make your healing different from what you have already tried.*

Trust core wound. *Not just trust of others but mistrust of self is huge.*

Trust your flow—the ups and downs. What is being denied you is for your highest good.

What you struggle to fix and save may not even be what you really want at the end of the day. Find yourself first, and then you'll know more of what you truly want. *This could be huge. Sit with this one.*

A rearranging of your life is going to occur.

Intuitive child. *You said both are.*

You are on autopilot. Involuntarily going through life. What do you want for you? What do you want to do for others? *When you are operating from your authentic self, what you do for you is what will be best for others. You don't always have to compromise what you want. Choose you. Lead by example.*

Parasite.

You don't have to stick with traditional values. You can create your own set of norms. *You said you already feel you do this. I think this is going to have a way deeper future meaning. So, sit with this, and see how it unfolds for you.*

Divine order. Heal you. Then, move outward and make major decisions from a place of clear sight. *I know you are a doer and want to make decisions and attack this, but the truth is you don't have to. You can allow yourself to start to heal, and from there you will organically know more of what you want and don't want. Then, you can more confidently make the decisions you want to make. When we heal, it's truly amazing how new people come into our lives at just the right time. And on the flip side, relationships that need to go organically slough away.*

Future worry. Preemptive worry. Keeps you out of the present. *Sent you homework on this.*

Crown chakra tingles. Intuitive. *You validated this.*

Protective energy.

Subconscious fear and worry. Learned behaviors that no longer serve you. Let these go. You are safe now. *You are still being led by things in your past that no longer serve you. Things that are buried deep in your subconscious. Uncover and unravel to heal.*

Not all soul connections are supposed to last a lifetime. It's ok to sever ties and create boundaries.

Mom—they had me circle her as being significant. *We chatted about your mom at length. Sometimes, when a person is fond of someone, they may not have an awareness that healing may need to occur. So, sit with this one. Journal.*

They are saying your mom has [certain tendencies], and thus you may have some of these tendencies. I do NOT want this to further label you, but just add this to your awareness. Remember the story of the boy and the butterfly. He was trying to help but harmed. We can unravel this one together, as this started some of the core wounds—or activated them.

You control so you don't have to self-trust. No margin for error. Trust your intuition. *Take baby steps to trust your intuition.*

You have some pretty amazing things that happen to you with Spirit. You have direct experiences with Divinity. So, try to trust more. Try to trust yourself—take baby steps, and then keep walking.

You can be successful and calm at the same time. Let your fight-or-flight rest. Clear sight is more accurate than when you're depleted.

Achievement—success void-filler of not enough, self-core wound. You are enough—stop feeding your core wound. *Practice non-attachment.*

Image.

What is your threshold for "enough?" *Sit with this one, and see what you come up with.*

You want change but you want to control it.

Tight.

Allow yourself to surrender, so you know what good really feels like.

Going in a lot of directions at once.

Release thoughts. Release past traumas that still control you. Let go. You may mentally, but also do it energetically. *We spoke of the importance of you releasing energies that don't serve you, once you have the awareness or heal a core wound. Core wounds don't go away but can become manageable. As you heal, release the energy from your mind and body. Set the intention. Ask the Divine. Talk to them. Use water. Whatever works for you.*

Are you fulfilled at your core?

Go to the root of the changes you want to implement. Why? Motivators?

Patterns—unravel.

UNWINDING PERFECT

I am here, I am here, I am here.
You are never alone- always protected.
Limiting beliefs are learned. They can be unlearned.

* * *

Well, then. That sure is a lot to unpack and unwind.

CHRISTINE CLYNE-SPRAKER

PART II

UNWINDING

Chapter 15

Perfectionism

"You don't have to control your thoughts. You just have to stop letting them control you."

—Dan Millman

WHAT'S INTERESTING ABOUT perfectionism is that, at least for me, I didn't really care if I was perfect. I didn't need a hundred percent on every test or to win every competition (although I do like to win!). I *did* need to be easygoing, please those I loved, not rock the boat, be fun and funny when I needed to be, and basically always on.

Perfectionism wasn't about being perfect. It was about never disappointing those I love. It was about sacrificing my feelings and my wants to be easygoing, so those around me got what they wanted. My value as a person was tied to my ability to please others, and I felt I had to be good and right to be worthy.

It felt unsafe to ask for what I wanted or needed, not because my parents intentionally made me feel unsafe, but because I had observed a chaotic familial environment, where family members who had strong opinions usually ended up fighting and talking loud and over one another. Sometimes, anger, slammed doors, or a phone being ripped out of the wall and thrown were known to occur. With little to no communication about the underlying issues that caused such behavior, it felt unsafe to me to have dissenting opinions or needs. It was safer to not ask at all.

According to the University of Maryland's Counseling Center website (https://counseling.umd.edu/cs):

> *Sometimes, when individuals experience insecurity, they seek validation and self-worth in their achievements, possibly leading to perfectionism. Others may feel a sense of insecurity not about who they are but about the world (due to difficult or uncontrollable factors in their lives) and turn to perfectionism to provide a sense of control.*
>
> *Perfectionism is a pattern of rigid and unrealistic thoughts, expectations, and behaviors with the intention of achieving excessively high goals and/or avoiding any mistakes, human flaws, or unplanned situations. Perfectionists often experience frustration, shame, disappointment, and self-blame when those expectations are not met. Additionally, perfectionism can cause frequent negative thoughts, worry, and self-doubt.*

By getting good grades and being "the easy child," I pleased my parents. By letting my sister, who loves me fiercely, also be incredibly mean to me at times, especially as I grew older, I devalued myself and learned that that is how love is showed. I didn't understand that this behavior wasn't healthy or that I had the right to tell her how she hurt me and/or to set boundaries. I allowed other people's labels of me, such as difficult or a know-it-all or toxic, to define me.

If I am too difficult, I better change my behavior.
Know too much? Shoot, I won't say that again.
Were my actions toxic? Yikes, I won't take a stand for myself.

By not knowing who I was and what my boundaries were, I constantly shapeshifted to meet the needs of everyone else, so as not to make them uncomfortable or to be seen critically by them.

Perfectionism is rooted in the incessant need to control, and since my control core wound dominated my life, I emerged with an A-type personality. It has been studied and demonstrated that "Type A women show greater autonomic arousal, time urgency and speed to laboratory stressors, more goal directedness, a preference to work alone under stress conditions, and more competitiveness/aggressiveness than Type B women." (Baker LJ et al, 1984.) I was all of those things.

As I grew older, the A-type aspect within me grew stronger. I always wanted to be the driver of a car in a group, because nothing made my nerves jump more than sitting in a car with a driver who wasn't angling to be first or the fastest. In my first job out of college, I had to be number one in *all* things, not just one or two of them. And when I was married with young kids and went traveling for work, the one thing I couldn't stand most was coming home to a messy and unorganized fridge full of leftover food that had been forgotten.

My need to control the outcome of situations and relationships, which subconsciously was to protect myself from intimacy, rejection, and abandonment, caused me to be the good girl who had no idea who I really was. This led to my other core wounds: lack of self and fear of abandonment. By not standing up for myself and what I wanted or desired, because I either didn't know what I really wanted or was so fearful the person would abandon me if I pushed too hard, I learned to be a chameleon and to want what everyone else wanted.

By always pleasing and not directly asking for what I wanted, it was difficult for people in my life to show up for me in my times of need. How could they? If I didn't know, or wasn't comfortable communicating my needs, they had zero shot at being able to meet them. Inadvertently, this led to a feeling of abandonment, and a vicious cycle perpetuated itself.

I know this now because Davie came into my life at the exact right time and became a friend and fierce ally. Even after the pandemic began, we continued to meet virtually about every three months. She helped me gain awareness and understanding of my behaviors and patterns and gave me tools to combat my core wounds as I slowly began to heal.

Chapter 16

Covid

"Rarely, if ever, are any of us healed in isolation. Healing is an act of communion."

—Bell Hooks

FOR MOST HUMANS ON this planet, Covid was full of surprising lessons. Some good and beautiful; others very hard and heartbreaking.

My family went into Covid when our daughter Isla was still very much a little girl. She wanted me to play with her, to use creative imagination, and to just hang out. One of my biggest regrets to this day is that I didn't make more time to do all of those things with her in those early months of the pandemic. While many health-tech companies were shuttering their doors due to the healthcare crisis, we were putting in extra hours to bring more value to our clients (hospitals), who were enduring unprecedented circumstances and being asked to perform damn-near miracles. The reality is I prioritized the business over my little girl.

I later realized that being creative and using my imagination with Isla made me uncomfortable. I had suppressed so much of the little girl inside me, and had never really had that type of relationship with my mom, that I simply didn't know how to naturally or easily connect.

Davie had said to me in our session, "People who sometimes may have some learned behaviors from having a loved one or parent [with your mother's tendencies] can learn to detach when they feel stress, fear, or worry coming on. Or loss of control. Sometimes, when the kids are struggling, the parent detaches in a way." I understand now that I detached because I didn't know any better, but my stomach still roils when I think about it.

Being creative and silly forced me to be intimate with her in ways I didn't know how to be, as well as vulnerable in a way I didn't know how to be. The imaginative and creative muscle wasn't something I had used much (outside of writing), which had kept me from really connecting at times with my little creator child, when she really needed it.

When it came to "doing" things, I was a very confident and a great mom. Want to go to the zoo and learn about animals? I'm in. Bake a cake or make dinner? I'm in. Go to the museum and talk about dinosaurs and body parts and space? I'm your gal.

Want to sit on the floor and use our imaginations and play? I'm… out. It was almost like a visceral response. I would throw myself into work, because I didn't know "how" to do some of the things our kids, especially Isla, wanted me to do. I let my left brain override my gut, and instead of being present and just flowing, I overthought it, made myself uncomfortable, and avoided situations that made me feel unsure of myself.

During the pandemic, I made sure the kids' daily virtual school was attended, I helped them with their schoolwork and homework, and we created some fun memories, including a family TikTok and family "date nights."

Each Wednesday, some combination of two of the four of us would cook dinner for the other two. We created a restaurant dining experience, and the two chefs served the two diners. My favorite night of all of them was the night when the two kids cooked for Josh and me. I think we had some combination of cooked noodles, cold red sauce, raw carrots, ranch, and bread.

But between the never-ending Covid days and the business's need for additional attention, I filled the long and empty Covid weeks on my computer working, instead of with Isla. She went into Covid as a nine-year old third grader and basically came out of Covid as a sixteen-year-old fifth grader. I say that jokingly, but the reality is, she was still a little girl when Covid started and was very much a young woman two years later. And by that time, creating and hanging with Mom was way less interesting than talking to her friends via FaceTime, creating TikTok dances, or playing Roblox. To this day, it is one of my biggest regrets that I couldn't throw myself into her the way she needed me to, the same way I threw myself into the business the way it needed me to.

I felt like I'd failed her, and it took a lot of work for me to let go of that guilt. Isla is a very enlightened young woman, and she actually helped me heal and let go of the guilt. Post-Covid, we had honest conversations about how I felt like I had let her down. Wise beyond her years, she is kind and gracious, and told me, "It's okay, Mommy. I am okay."

* * *

Despite my guilt and feeling like I failed Isla, I was more present with my kids during Covid than I had been in years. In addition, our son Mason, who was in fourth grade when the pandemic started, thrived. He was able to experience new freedoms and adventures, including riding his bike through the neighborhood, and he got a phone so we could track him. He reflects on Covid as some of the best years of his young life. It's interesting how two children in the same household can have two totally opposite experiences during a major world event.

* * *

Each of us has learned behaviors, mostly inherited from our parents, starting from a young age. I know I learned to disconnect from intimacy from my mom, and even as a child, it was hard for me to be vulnerable, silly, goofy, messy, or whatever didn't appear as perfect. Many of her tendencies became my tendencies.

My mom, whom I adore and seriously thought wore a halo most of my life, wasn't perfect. But it took me a long time to figure that out. And it's hard for her, quite frankly, to know who she is, after so many years of putting on a happy face and not asking for her needs to be met.

She projected this idea of perfectionism: don't show emotions (other than everything is okay), create the perfect house and life, and don't ever really get too close emotionally to anyone. Including your children. Do "all the things" for them, but don't be vulnerable. Don't have hard conversations that might make them uncomfortable (or, worse, make *you* uncomfortable!). Be a tight unit with your spouse, go to church, and don't dream of anything too big.

I started to ask myself, if all of these behaviors are learned, does that mean I could also reverse the same behaviors? By simply bringing attention and awareness to them, could I start to behave differently? What if I no longer cared about showcasing perfect? What if I was exhausted and unfulfilled from the pursuit? Could I actually learn to be "un-perfect?" To be messy, emotional, vulnerable, and, heaven forbid…too much?

Chapter 17

Diane Von Furstenberg

"I wanted to be an empowered woman, and I became an empowered woman. And now, I want to empower every woman. And I do it through my clothes, I do it through my words, I do it through my money. I do it through everything."

—Diane Von Furstenberg

ONE OF THE BOOKS I read during Covid was Diane von Furstenberg's *The Woman I Wanted to Be*. Until her book, I had never heard a woman speak the way she did. The confidence she had in herself and the way she made decisions that were best for her—it was empowering, and it awakened my soul.

She didn't make her decisions because they were what her first husband wanted. No, she made them for herself. She didn't even make decisions for her children. Nor for the man she loved, with whom she had an on-again, off-again relationship for many years before eventually marrying him. She lived for herself. Confidently and unapologetically.

Because of this, she showed up as a better mom and partner to those she loved. She didn't waiver in the ambiguity of should she/shouldn't she. She listened to her gut and was secure in what she stood for. She knew, even if her decisions hurt other people's feelings or led to the loss of a relationship, she was following her heart and would be okay.

I knew right then and there that I needed to be more like DVF and much less of the people-pleaser I had been most of my life. I knew, for me to create a more fulfilling life that included putting my needs first, I would have to channel my inner DVF. And I knew, by making choices that were from my heart, I would ultimately become a better role model for our children.

And so, I started.

On September 28, 2020, I was writing in my journal about something that had happened and how proud I was of myself for not letting the situation define me. I wrote,

> *I don't know what the future holds. Love-wise. Career-wise. But I'm open to happiness. And creating joy. Joy in my heart, and joy all around me. Joy is the expression of love. And I have so much love to give. And I am excited to receive. I'm open to it. I surrender.*
>
> *I no longer wish to control outcomes. For so many, 2020 has been a year of suffering and crisis. For me, it's been a year of new opportunities. A new way to see myself, both my flaws and my strengths. To trust myself. To stand up and demand what I think is fair. The quietness has brought the opportunity to connect with myself. To slow down. To figure out what is real. What is my truth. I still am not 100% on what my truth will become. But I know major change needs to occur. A massive shift.*

My health is getting better. I'm not working as much as I was. And I will approach everything with love.

I am so grateful to DVF, a woman I have never met.

I used to feel ashamed or embarrassed about certain choices. But through her book and her raw honesty about her love of life, I realized it's all okay.

I'm loving the woman I'm becoming.

Before that day, I don't know if I had ever really held love for myself. I liked myself enough. I knew I had some great qualities, and I was proud of my accomplishments. But I never seemed to be enough, or right, for the people in my life. And the constant critic in my head would criticize the one wrong thing I did, instead of celebrate the ten great things I did.

The other thing about reading DVF's book is that it was the first book I had read for my own enjoyment in years. Instead of reading for pleasure, I had been reading for survival—business acumen acquisition, honing leadership skills, strategy from successful businessmen (every business book I read outside of Sheryl Sandberg's *Lean In* was written by a man), and books about different financing options, so I would be fully prepared for future capital events.

2020 sparked something new in me. A glimmer of hope. An understanding that the situation I was in was not who I was. That I had power and ability to create change. And as much as I loved my life, my family, and the business, I realized, more than anything, it was comfortable. I was comfortable in the family unit my husband and I had created and comfortable in the social dynamics of our unit. This included with friends and family.

Comfortable didn't equate to happiness or fulfillment.

As I started to unwind some of the conditioned patterns that had created the machine I had become—wake, early-morning work meeting, emails, breakfast for kids, drop at school, work, work, work, work, dinner, maybe a game or walk around the neighborhood, more email, bed, wake, and do it all over again—I became less of a machine and more aware of the void-fillers I turned to when I was lonely, sad, disappointed, etc. It allowed me to hold space for the fact that I really wasn't happy.

And I knew I wanted to be happy and find joy. I knew I wanted more for my life, for my children, and for my relationships. I was starting to gain courage to ask for what I wanted and needed, and instead of feeling stuck, I was beginning to feel empowered.

Chapter 18

Hard Conversations

"Truthfulness is the foundation of all human virtues."
—Abdu'l-Bahá

PART OF CHOOSING YOURSELF means first starting to understand what aspects of your life serve your highest good and what aspects are no longer serving you. This is scary for many reasons. It's scary because you get to start thinking about yourself and what your hopes and dreams might be. But it's also scary because, once you start filtering, it means inevitable change. Once you have awareness, it's impossible to turn your back on what you now know.

When you start putting yourself first, people in your life are going to go. Bad habits are going to go. Things that feel like a security blanket are going to be ripped away from you. But it doesn't have to be bad, and it doesn't have to be mean. It will be scary. And it will be hard. But the people who truly love you will understand. Conversely, the people who love how you show up for them and who benefit from your lack of boundaries won't understand. Both are okay. You must be willing to let go of the bad to let in more of the good.

Once you start to get clear on what is important to you, you can't really go back. I mean, you can, but you have this knowing that there is something more for you. That you deserve more. And that knowing and that feeling become overwhelming. When that clarity begins to surface, you have two choices: inaction or action.

Inaction means doing nothing.

Action means having hard conversations with the people you love. You know it might hurt or surprise them or that, potentially, things might change. But you can't let it stop you. Because, if it does, you risk not stepping into your true self. And you risk not realizing a true contentment and joy we are all destined to achieve, if we allow for it.

When you let go of fear and realize you are not responsible for how someone responds to you and it is not your job to try to convince them of who you are, you are empowered to make choices that best benefit you. You will never be wrong when you are honest with yourself and come from a place of truth.

Not that any of this was easy for me. Initially, it was terrifying. I had built my entire life upon a foundation of pleasing and meeting others' needs, and the thought of disappointing someone or hurting them felt repugnant. Over time, setting boundaries and speaking my truth became easier, but intuitively I knew I was about to blow my whole comfortable life up, which scared me to death.

The courage for me to speak my truth didn't happen overnight, and I didn't feel courageous at all. I was scared, heartbroken, and saddened by the fact that what I had wanted out of my life had not come to fruition. That I was desperate for intimate relationships and had none, but also fully aware it was a result of who and what I had chosen. Me finding my truth and starting to understand what truly served me did not happen overnight. It was a journey that had started years before, and I had been taking baby steps toward. Now, I was ready (or more ready, anyway) to leap.

Having hard conversations was not a skill I had learned as a child, nor something I was comfortable doing. My family swept hurt feelings or bad behavior under the rug and acted like nothing had ever happened. The only time we had serious talks were when we broke rules and got caught. Then, there were big lessons, and the fear of disappointing Mom and Dad was pretty much punishment in and of itself.

How to have hard conversations around feelings, expectations, and boundaries was not a skillset I had. In the past, when I tried to have hard conversations about my wants or needs, I often felt shut down or not validated by the person I was trying to have the conversation with. I didn't have the skills to navigate the conversation or the self-worth and value to understand that my feelings deserved to be heard.

My experiences led to a cycle where it became easier not to advocate for myself. Sometimes, my feelings were flipped on me, and suddenly I was the problem. Instead of having a safe place to express how I felt with someone who truly sought to understand my feelings, it became the opposite. I later learned this is a form of emotional abuse and a tactic used by other wounded individuals who are unable to cope with their own insecurities when they arise. But it wasn't until I gained strength in myself, in who I was and what I valued, that I was able to begin these hard conversations.

And I didn't learn the skill of hard conversations until my time as co-CEO. At first, it scared me to death, and I couldn't stand the thought of hurting someone's feelings or being brutally honest with them. Even with employees, who benefitted from critical feedback. I credit my former business partner with helping me learn to navigate such situations. And somewhere along the way, I was introduced to the book, *Never Kick a Cow Chip on a Hot Day* by Todd Ordal.

The book's premise is about the importance of being *kind* over *nice*. Todd argues in his book that when you are nice, you are being agreeable and avoiding difficult topics. While the recipient of your niceness may feel warm and fuzzy, you are not giving them an opportunity to glean awareness in a situation that might help them grow. On the other hand, being kind means making yourself uncomfortable to give the recipient the opportunity to learn, grow, change, or any of the other valuable lessons that may occur.

Reframing critical feedback and hard conversations as a benefit rather than a negative helped me shift my approach and allowed me to share more freely. Professionally, I began to navigate complicated situations with much more ease, and the worry I had about hurting someone's feelings dissipated. I started to gain more and more experience, and it naturally just became easier.

Despite the practice I was getting at work having hard conversations, I was not prepared to bring this new skill into my personal life. The people in my personal life were used to me behaving a certain way, and changing how I showed up to them was frightening. It meant showing up in a different way, being uncomfortable, and making those I love feel uncomfortable. Eventually, I learned that the more I was willing to step into these hard conversations and start speaking my truth, the easier they became. I became more convicted.

In the fall of 2020, I finally started to accept the fact that my marriage had very little chance of survival. We were two trains on two different tracks, going to two totally different stations. The one thing holding us together were our kids, while the things that were missing began to take on more weight. This included a deep connection, a true bond, and a willingness to continue fighting. I could no longer settle for the imbalance. As much as I wanted to keep our family unit together for our kids, I yearned for something more. More real and more connected.

I finally got up the courage to talk to Josh about my feelings one night; about where my head was at and how unhappy I had become. I shared with him a few things I needed from him in order for us to have a shot at staying together. I was nervous and my voice shook, as I told him. But I did it. I put myself out there in a way I had been unable to do before. I was clear on what I needed, and I communicated it to him.

On September 25, 2020, I wrote,

> *I have been very open with Josh this last week, no longer fearful of the ramifications of telling him how I feel. I told him I have been unhappy for a long time. And that I'm tired. And while I'm not mad at him anymore, I don't know how to be close to him. Or how we become close*

again. I'm sad. I love him, he has been my husband for 13 years. But I feel in my bones it's time to move on.

Around this same time, we were supposed to go to Napa Valley with some friends. We had gone in January 2020, and it had been such an amazing trip, we booked it again for the fall. Only this time, it didn't feel right to me. Instead of looking forward to the wine tasting and late nights, I dreaded it. I was exhausted just thinking about it and almost panicked about the thought of going.

About a week before the trip, I called my mom in tears as I left the office. I couldn't explain it, other than I was exhausted and the thought of the trip was putting me over the edge. In hindsight, I was processing so much about my life, who I was becoming, and my relationships, the thought of consuming alcohol with a group of friends and a man with whom I wasn't sure where our relationship was headed sounded 180-degrees opposite from what I wanted. I had an inner knowing, a feeling. Staying home was exactly what I needed.

On the phone with my mom that day, I decided not to go. This was a big decision for me, because I knew I would disappoint people, and being the perpetual people-pleaser, I didn't want to let anyone down.

My mom had already agreed to watch our kids that weekend, and on the phone, we decided she would still take them. That would give me a weekend at home, by myself, and allow me time to rest and decompress. I was instantly relieved, and the tightness I had been feeling in my body began to loosen. I had chosen myself, and my body responded with gratitude. This was the first positive visceral reaction I could remember having in a very long time. I would learn, over the next couple of years, that by listening to my body, I could begin to trust myself in times when I was unsure.

Through all of this, I had kept the stress of my marriage and its potential fallout from my mom and my dad. I didn't talk about it at all with them. They adored Josh and to this day still think of him as a son. Because of this, I never felt like I was truly able to share with them our struggles. This only compounded my stress and anxiety about making such a monumental decision about our marriage.

The other thing that happened on the phone with my mom that day was that she made me promise to book a long weekend at a wellness resort. There was a resort I had been talking about for a couple of years, but for one reason or another had never prioritized it for myself. When I went home, I cried, telling Josh I wasn't going to Napa. I felt selfish, and I felt guilty that he would now be a fifth wheel. I texted our friends to tell them and felt more guilt. That weekend, while I was home alone, I booked a solo trip over my forty-first birthday for four-nights at Mii amo in Sedona, Arizona, and that night, instead of guilt, I felt anticipation.

I learned a funny lesson that weekend, while I was home, Josh was in Napa, and our kids were with my parents. When you take time to listen to your body and your gut, miracles will occur. Because I was home, I got to spend that weekend with our sweet twelve-year-old Goldendoodle, Molly, who had been diagnosed with bone cancer in March and had had her front right leg amputated in July. She stopped eating and drinking the weekend I was home alone with her. I knew it was time to say goodbye after she weakly took herself outside on Saturday night to lie in the grass and stare up at the sky for a few hours. I called Josh and told him, and we decided we would say goodbye to her when he and the kids got home the next day.

A very wonderful woman came to our house and performed in-home euthanasia. It was beautiful, and I am grateful to her for her services. We all got to love on Molly, while she lay on her favorite dog bed and peacefully went to sleep for the last time.

Years earlier, in 2016, when Josh and I had had to put down our then nine-year old beloved Goldendoodle, Dixie, in the vet's office, I was stone cold. I had hardened so much, I couldn't allow myself to cry or feel the pain of Dixie's loss. But as Molly slowly began to take her last breaths, I bawled. I cried my eyes out. And then cried more later.

It took my kids by surprise. They were not used to seeing me upset, but it also gave them permission to feel their emotions. Like my parents, I had not done a great job demonstrating emotions other than everything is okay. Molly gave me permission to cry. I gave myself permission to cry. She had become my dog and my protector after Dixie died, and I will be forever grateful that I was able to be home with her that last weekend.

Chapter 19

Leading with Love

"The soul's experience on Earth is not meant for hard work and toil. It's meant for freedom, ease, and expansion."
—Vishen Lakhiani, *The Buddha and the Badass*

SOMETIME DURING THE FALL of 2020, I really started to hit a new groove. The self-critic in my head was beginning to quiet, the fabric of my control core wound was thinning, and I was living less to please others and more to meet my own needs. In turn, I was showing up happier, more confident, and as a better mom, partner, friend, etc. I was stepping into what it meant to own my intelligence and appearance—both of which I had played down much of my life, to make others (mainly men) feel more confident and comfortable around me. I was owning my role as co-CEO, leading important presentations and conversations, and confidently speaking up about strategic business decisions.

I believe fully that the universe will put the right information in front of you at the right time, a theme I began to see play out repeatedly the more open and less rigid I became. In this particular instance, the book *The Buddha and the Badass: The*

Secret Spiritual Art of Succeeding at Work found me. I loved this book. It was as if the author, Vishen Lakhiani, knew how to take the intangible, abstract from my brain, and put it into written word. I loved his book and pictured myself growing in both my spirituality and badass-ness when I read it.

The back cover promised: "Uncover your soulprint, attract your allies, become unf*ckwithable, activate your inner visionary, build a unified brain, upgrade your identity, bend reality..." For me, the biggest takeaway from the book was very simple: lead with love. Allow love to seep into every crevice of your business.

The idea of leading with love was not foreign to me: it was something I had done for most of my professional career. When I was an assistant manager at Enterprise Rent-a-Car, I loved my employees and encouraged joyful expression in everyday branch life. As a regional sales director in medical device sales, I baked homemade cookies for my customers and delivered them with genuine excitement. My true authentic self had always been bursting with love, and I had so much to share.

But somewhere along the way, I had hardened. The stress of the business increased. The busyness of school-age children and their related activities, school functions, and endless birthday parties was constant. And I had shifted from being an open and carefree woman to an unhappy, tightly wound, business-all-the-time person.

While reading *The Buddha and the Badass*, I decided I didn't want to be that person anymore. I wanted to lead with love, both professionally and personally. I wanted to create more experiences for all the people in my life, and I wanted to create more experiences for myself. I wanted to find joy again…, along with easy, belly-shaking laughter. More than anything, I wanted to laugh again.

The Buddha and the Badass also reminded me about daily positive affirmations. Each morning, I would tap in at a minimum three times, but often more, "Today, I will grow myself, and I will grow my business." As the habit of repeating mantras once again became ingrained in my daily routine, so did the expansion of my mantras.

On days when I was feeling especially dejected as a mother, I would tap in, "I'm a great mom. I'm a great mom. I'm a great mom." Or, if I was nervous for an upcoming presentation, "I'm a great speaker. I'm a great speaker. I'm a great speaker." My inner critic quieted, and the positive focus on components of my life that I'd previously held insecurities about began to dissipate.

As I was rereading my journals in preparation for this book, I noticed something else was subconsciously taking place in my writing. There was a dramatic change in the tone of my journals as my self-discovery journey progressed. Before 2020, the entries were sad and self-critical, filled with lack of self and a desperate need for external validation. Guilt over the "should haves" with my children. Constant back-and-forth drama of, "Do I do this?" or "Do I do that?" never with any courage to step into what my gut clearly was screaming that it wanted. There was so much fear. So much control.

But as I continued to read my journals while I prepped for each new chapter, the tone changed. The critic began to go away. The self-love and appreciation for myself began to grow. I couldn't quite let go of some of my lack-of-self core wound that led to my constant concern with feeling respected… but even it was easing.

On October 23, 2020, I wrote,

> *I'm so excited for my Mii amo trip. I'm going to rest. I'm going to read, and I'm going to meditate. I'm going to be open to new experiences with zero expectation or control of the outcome. I'm flowing with life, and I love it. I feel like the control side of me is completely gone. Or me trying to control an outcome is gone. But I have this weird feeling that I need to see Zoe or Davie. I feel like there is something I am missing. A small key to unlock what is next. I'm happy today. I'm focused on being present. On joy. On operator excellence.*
>
> *I love my kids.*
>
> *Sooooooo much.*
>
> *And I realized I let go of something last night—all this guilt I have about yelling so much when they were younger and feeling like an inadequate mom. It's probably not even as bad as I remember it. And what if me being gone [traveling all the time] made them wildly independent? And what if the guilt really has no reason to feel guilty for?*

By beginning to let go of guilt and shame and the patterns that had formed my behaviors but no longer served me, I was beginning to let new in. New ways of showing up in the world that were more authentic and aligned to my true self.

In turn, I was more comfortable in my own skin and more able to show up for my people in the ways they actually needed me to. As my true self. A self that showed up from a place that I needed, instead of a place I thought others around me needed. I was more authentic and more myself with my kids, my friends, my family, and all the amazing employees I worked with.

Chapter 20

Signs

"Life is a song—sing it. Life is a game—play it. Life is a challenge—meet it. Life is a dream—realize it. Life is love—enjoy it."

—Sai Baba

WHILE I WAS FEELING stronger about owning my feelings and communicating them, I still didn't fully trust myself that certain wants or needs I had were valid. I felt selfish for even considering a divorce. What if it was the wrong decision? What if I regretted it? What if our kids never recovered? The "what if's" played over and over in my head, and I wrote in my journal at one point, "I need a break from my mind, lol." It was exhausting. I didn't trust myself, and I thought I had to have everything planned out and controlled for.

In mid-2020, Davie taught me how to ask for signs when I needed confirmation about something I was unsure of in my life. She told me to be very clear and intentional about what I needed clarity on. Then, she said, ask for a specific sign within a specific timeframe. If you see the sign, it validates your question. If the sign does not appear, it negates your question.

I was very skeptical, mostly because I had never thought of myself as a conduit to receive messages or signs from the metaphysical world. After asking for some specific signs and not receiving them (only later to realize not receiving the sign I'd asked for was the answer to the questions I had asked), I was even more skeptical.

I was so skeptical that, one day in August 2020, I asked my spiritual guides to show me a sign if I could see signs. I specifically asked to be shown a rainbow in the next forty-eight hours.

When I woke up that next morning and went downstairs, the family room TV was on. And not on a cable channel or the smart TV home screen. It was as if some input had been adjusted, moving from our regular channels to whatever this was. On the screen looked like a planet in a universe of stars, with refracted light filtering down upon it in the colors of a rainbow. I was mesmerized and also terrified. I knew the TV had not been on when I went to bed the night before, and it seemed so far out there, I couldn't believe it was the rainbow sign I had asked for.

For the rest of the day, odd electronic disturbances continued to occur. For example, Isla had a doctor's appointment, and as we drove to it, we were playing Taylor Swift from my phone through the car's speakers. As we sang along, the most bizarre thing happened. The speakers cut from the song to a really loud, staticky noise—it didn't even sound like it was coming from my speakers. You could faintly make out it was the same song, but it sounded like a dead, crackling radio channel was playing over the streaming music.

I looked at Isla. She looked at me with concern in her eyes, and we immediately shut off the radio. I admitted to my daughter right then that I had asked for a sign from the universe to show me if I could see signs, and she agreed that what had just happened *was* an incredible sign. The hair on my arms stood up.

Later that day, I was on a virtual meeting with an employee, and all of a sudden, she goes, "Whoa, what was that? That sound is so weird."

I couldn't hear it, but she described how I'd sounded, coming through the speakers, as exactly like what Isla and I heard during the Taylor Swift song earlier that day.

The electronic interference was obviously not the rainbow I had asked for originally. But the TV coming on with the refracted rainbow light on screen was too coincidental to ignore. And then, the additional electronic occurrences during that day made me wonder if I had now cultivated a new language with my spiritual team.

That same night, as I was helping Isla search for something in her room, I saw a rainbow of pipe cleaners on her shelf in her closet. I finally allowed myself the recognition that I'd seen a sign. The rainbow I had asked for was shown to me in a very obvious way. And then, it didn't stop.

As I was brushing Isla's hair, I realized she had worn a bow to gymnastics, one she hadn't worn in over a year—and there were rainbows all over it. As I looked at the pile of clothes on her floor from the day, I realized she had also worn a leotard to gymnastics with rainbows all over it. I suddenly realized, by simply being present and aware, I was completely open to signs.

Over the next several months, in a separate journal, I continued to track signs that I asked for. I was still so in my head, while unwinding all of my previous patterns, I needed to continue to prove the power of the universe to myself; not only my ability to tap into it, but also that my gut instincts, around which I was still asking for clarity, were actually accurate.

Over time, as my head and heart became more coherent, I simply began to trust myself more, and the need to validate my instincts became less important. But those first few months were pivotal as I learned a new language with the universe. While signs continue to play a big role in my life, especially when I am at a significant crossroads, I also know that the impulses I feel deep within my body are more than a whim. They are an inner knowing that go far beyond anything we can conjure up in our minds. These impulses are not something we are meant to ignore.

UNWINDING PERFECT

Chapter 21

Sedona

"Thank God for granting me this moment of clarity, this moment of honesty. The world'll feel my truths."
—Jay-Z, "Moment of Clarity," *The Black Album*

IN NOVEMBER 2020, I spent five days alone in Sedona, Arizona. I had no agenda other than to receive exactly what I was supposed to receive in those five days. I had carefully looked over the spa menu and indulgently scheduled six services over the course of my stay. I was intentional to make sure I left plenty of time to hike, rest, and meditate. I was the only solo traveler staying in the Mii amo casitas—everyone else there had chosen to travel and stay with a partner. Unlike them, I was seeking solitude, clarity, and solace.

At Mii amo, a spa and private casita lodging on the Enchantment Resort property, I basked in the glory of beautiful self-discovery, through soul-awakening spa services that included hypnosis, a chakra vibrational massage, integrative breathing, full-body scrub, tarot reading, and a Thai massage with energy clearing. The services alone were restorative and healing. But while I was there in Boynton Canyon, an ancient healing ground that includes a purported energy vortex at Kachina Woman Rock just a short hike from the Mii amo spa, I experienced many miracles.

As I allowed myself to become more introspective and reflective about my patterning, mannerisms, defense mechanisms, etc., I was also becoming more present and more aware. My biggest uncertainty was my marriage. The questions, "Do I, or don't I?" and "When?" repeatedly cycled through my head. My hope was that my time in Boynton Canyon would offer some clarity.

My friend Emily, who had visited Mii amo, had brought me back a heart-shaped stone made of the hard-packed red clay for which Sedona is famous. She had shared with me that there was a flute-player named Robert who played music atop the canyon at the heart of the vortex. He often offered spirit-guided messages and a heart clay stone to hikers, as they passed through.

When I got to Mii amo on Sunday, I thought, well, maybe I'll ask for a sign, and if I'm supposed to have the divorce conversation with Josh when I get back, the flute-player will give me a message.

I heard Robert's flute several times during my stay in Sedona. However, as many times as I hiked up to the Kachina Woman Rock, I never saw him. I thought it was strange that I had not run into him, and maybe that I was a little crazy. But I also had this weird gut feeling that, even if I did see him, he wasn't going to share a message with me. (I later realized it had not been the right timing for me to discuss a divorce with Josh, and hence why I never was able to run into Robert).

UNWINDING PERFECT

By Tuesday, after experiencing several ah-ha moments during my spa services, I was fairly confident I had internally worked through the answer to my question. I decided to ask for another sign, but this time to a very different question.

Both Tammy and Davie had shared with me at different times that my life was currently on Plan A, and if I had the courage to trust Life, there was also an incredibly beautiful Plan B. Plan B was an alternative path that led to self-love, peace, and joy, unlike anything I had experienced before. So, this time, when I asked for a sign, I asked for a yellow butterfly to be shown to me by Thursday, before I left Mii amo, if Plan B included Josh and me separating.

Since it was fall in Sedona, the leaves were turning and the air was crisper, so butterflies were not something I had seen. I wanted the sign to be big, obvious, and in my face.

By Wednesday of my trip, I had almost fully relaxed; I had stopped looking at email and finally surrendered to the idea of not being so scheduled. On Monday and Tuesday, I had been very intentional about the timing of my services, so I could make use of every minute in Boynton Canyon. I had once again overscheduled myself, similar to what I did in my everyday life back home. I rushed from a sunrise hike to breakfast to my first session, back to the trails, and then to my next session..., without allowing myself the grace to just be and to be present.

But by Wednesday, I was ready to flow.

As I was heading out to hike the Boynton Canyon Trail, a roughly seven-mile out-and-back hike, I bumped into the Mii amo general manager. He casually mentioned to keep a lookout for acorn woodpeckers. He said I would know I found them when

I saw a tree with well-bored holes in it, where the birds stored acorns away from other animals. I thanked him for the tip and made a mental note of where he'd said to look for the tree.

The previous days, I had hiked the short Boynton Vista Trail above Mii amo to reach Kachina Woman Rock and the fabled vortex energy. I had ventured north and around the bend of the resort each day, but never much farther on the Boynton Canyon Trail. This day, I was determined to follow the trail to its end and not be in a rush. Additionally, I now had the added adventure of looking for the acorn woodpeckers.

While the true trailhead began south of the resort, at a public parking lot, there were two convenient ways to join the trail from the resort. The most northern resort entry had two curious features where the trail and the resort converged. The first was a squadron of javelinas who visited daily. They appeared throughout the day, grazing in the valley and around the green grass on the resort property. While mostly harmless, the wild animals would leave you alone, if you left them alone.

The second curious encounter, right before you merge onto the trail, was coming across four large, colorful, rough-cut wooden crosses set in a circle. One is black, one is white, one is blue, and one is yellow. Just beyond the crosses, another path led to a small Native American altar, where hundreds of small gifts had been left. I promised myself I would stop on my return from the hike to leave a small token of my appreciation.

I set off on my way. Unlike the previous days' hikes, when I was rushing to get as far as I could as quickly as I could, on this hike, I took my time. I slowed my pace and opened my senses.

I listened for the drum of a woodpecker. I relished in the beauty of Sedona's fall aspen trees—not quite red like turning Colorado aspen; more a beautiful pink hue that seemed to set the horizon on fire. I touched trees that had been struck by lightning and felt the warmth of the sun on my skin. I was present. I was alive. And I had nowhere to be.

I recalled in my journal later that night:

November 4th, 2020

One of my favorite lessons I have learned here is the awareness about my constant rush from one thing to the next. I cram way too much into my everyday life. I completely miss everything going on around me.

Lose the agenda.

Lose owing anyone anything.

Flow.

I had been disappointed on the hike's ascent, when I couldn't find the acorn woodpecker tree. I had followed the GM's directions but somehow had missed the turnoff.

I made it to the end of the trail, where I paused and enjoyed the view from a massive rock jutting out from the side of the mountain, which created a natural stadium-seating formation. I sat and ate the sandwich I had packed, then took time for a small meditation and moment of gratitude.

I had run into one of the couples who had traveled in on the same day as I had and stopped to chat with them. Normally, I would be in such a rush, I would politely say hi, but not stop to really engage, for fear the minutes used would make me late to my next whatever.

They shared with me that they both were remarried and as happy as could be. They had well-adjusted children and grandchildren. I was particularly interested in learning this, because I was seeking that clarity around the future of my marriage, how children adjust to divorce, and second chances at love.

I knew I was grossly unhappy, and I knew Josh was unhappy. And I knew, in those moments when I was really honest with myself, our marriage was over. But I didn't know how. Or when. And as a planner and doer, the indecision and grayness of it all was slowly killing me. I had yet to truly understand the duality of life and the need to sometimes just balance in the ambiguity of limbo. The limbo made me so uncomfortable that I'd learned to cope by making fast decisions and acting on them. It made me very successful in my career but was a horrible recipe for self-reflection and coping with hard emotions.

And this wasn't my career. My marriage and our family life were different, and there were two beautiful, innocent children whose hearts I couldn't bear the thought of hurting. I couldn't make a rash decision, and the fear of regretting my decision was almost intolerable. Like my purgatory in the wake of Bear's death, I was terrified I would "just decide to do it," and then it would be too late.

How does one go from being a wife of thirteen years (at the time) to a divorced mother of two? How does one unwind a "perfect" life?

Each time I thought about my children and not being with them 100% of the time, my heart broke. And then, it would break again into a million small pieces at the mere thought of even telling our kids we were not going to be together anymore. The battle continued to rage deep within me. While I was bringing more peace and certainty into some aspects of my life, the "how to handle my marriage" war silently waged on in my head.

As I walked away from the couple, the husband said to me, "You know, you both give all your energy and feel like you get nothing in return. It's exhausting."

I nodded in agreement and thought deeply about that statement as I climbed back down the mountain. So often, I felt like Josh and I both thought we were giving each other roses, but we were both just giving the other person sad, cheap bunches of carnations. And it *was* exhausting. Always feeling like you are giving roses and getting carnations in return.

As I thought about his words on my descent, I stopped suddenly. Was that a woodpecker I heard in the distance? I looked to my left and saw leaves fall to the ground. I didn't hear the pecking anymore, but I walked to where the leaves had dropped. And I listened.

Suddenly, a little farther in the distance, I heard it again. I looked around and saw the woodpecker atop a gigantic old, leafless, branchless, and most likely dead tree. And he had a mate. The two of them sat atop that tree and tirelessly worked to bore their holes.

As I examined the tree, I saw there were literally thousands of holes in it, and I began taking what seemed like thousands of pictures. I felt like a kid who had just found the last clue to a treasure hunt, where the birds and the tree were the treasure.

I was elated.

I relished in the glory of discovering the woodpeckers and the beautiful tree that sustained them. I felt happy about being present, using my senses during the beautiful hike that day to explore the beauty of Boynton Canyon and taking it all in. And to not be rushing. To take my time, to feel the sunshine on my skin. To be alive.

I meandered back onto the property, still high from finding the woodpeckers and thinking about how beautiful the world was when I was open and present. My heart, my senses, my childlike curiosity. And as I neared my casita, the most beautiful, and very large, yellow and black butterfly flew directly in front of me, circled me once, and then flew off in the direction I had just come from. I stopped, unsure at first that what I had just seen was real. But it was, and it was my sign.

I immediately began to sob. I cried tears of joy for the experience I had just had with the butterfly. I cried tears of sorrow for the sign that had just validated what I knew deep within me but was too afraid to admit. I cried for the loss of my marriage and for the two amazing humans I was so worried about hurting. And I cried for me. The years of being alone, a robot, of going through the motions, the exhaustion. The lack of self. I knew, at that moment, my life would be forever changed. There was no going back.

When I finally got back to my room and contemplated my day, I realized I had felt something that day that I hadn't felt in a really long time.

Joy.

I felt pure joy. I had opened myself to the beauty of nature. I had listened to myself for what I truly needed in the moment that day. And an inner knowing deep inside me, which I had tried to ignore for a very long time, was validated.

I wrote in my journal that night,

November 4, 2020

I felt joy again for the first time in… when? Forever, it seems.

Chapter 22

Permission

"Start with what is right rather than what is acceptable."
—Franz Kafka

December 29, 2020

It's the sunsetting of what many call the worst year ever. Covid sucks—but it could have been so much worse for us. I think of all the new wisdom and self-reflection I was able to find this year. The clarity. 2020 vision?

I'm grateful for this year. It has forced me to go inward and fix some of my major flaws. And get okay with not being okay. To be okay about change. To be okay about opportunity.

IF 2020 WAS A YEAR of clarity, then 2021 was a year of action. My inner strength and confidence were growing by the day. The business had survived Covid and was growing. Energetically, I was shifting from "always on" to "not always on as much."

Although it was still unclear what the future held for Josh and me, we decided to move forward with architectural plans for a new property we had purchased in 2020. And most importantly, our kids were finally back in the classroom after eleven months of being home. We were able to book two family vacations, the first with my parents and sister to our favorite lake in Georgia, and the second to Antigua, a trip we had postponed from June 2020.

I decided in January 2021 that I was going to write a book. I had always loved writing, and by that time, several of my mentors had confirmed my inkling that writing would be very good for me. Plus, I saw how brilliantly Vishen marketed MindValley with *The Buddha and the Badass,* and I began to catch on to how a book could potentially be used as a marketing tool for our business.

I was fascinated by the fact that healthcare stakeholders, such as health insurance companies, healthcare systems, and doctors, didn't have aligned incentives for optimal, cost-effective patient care. Healthcare is a business, and like any business, its fiduciary responsibility is to earn profits. But because the stakeholder incentives are contradictory to the other stakeholders' interests, the United States spends more money on healthcare than any other developed country, yet has the worst outcomes compared to any other developed country. Patients lose, and the sad fact is that not one stakeholder's forecast or budget includes a *patient* cell in the Excel formula. Patients are virtually excluded in the business of healthcare.

The enormity of this problem made headlines after Berkshire Hathaway, JP Morgan Chase, and Amazon tried to disrupt the healthcare industry by forming Haven. Haven was a not-for-profit healthcare entity intended to reduce healthcare costs and improve outcomes for employees of the joint venture. After failing to deliver on Haven's vision, the joint venture was disbanded, and Warren Buffett, chairman and CEO of Berkshire Hathaway, called the U.S. healthcare system a tapeworm in the American economy. Healthcare accounts for seventeen percent of the United States's GDP with little likelihood of that number ever being reduced.

So, I thought I would write a book about the misaligned and pervasive incentives in healthcare, and what our company was contributing to help reduce the problem. I started creating outlines of chapters and traded in my regular journaling for a daily accountability planner.

I started with the "goal-focused, time-based, and actionable" *Self Journal* daily planner in January 2021. The *Self Journal* is a thirteen-week journal/planner structured to help you reach short-term goals, create and track daily habits to help reach these goals and larger goals, and allow for reflection of your actions taken. I thought I could use its structure to help me prioritize writing the book, along with my business and familial obligations.

I went strong for six weeks, but somewhere around mid-February, I fell off, and that was my last entry in that *Self Journal*.

Looking back and reading the journal, it's clear I was unable to transition my life to become more narrowly focused. I allowed myself to be distracted and pulled in a million directions. I never wrote one word for that book, even after creating notes and early concepting ideas. Despite the journal failure and not accomplishing my goal to write the book, I was falling more in love with my job and role every day. I was finally thriving as a co-

CEO, and I loved the confidence I was gaining. I loved the woman I was becoming.

In March, we took our family spring break trip to Lake Oconee, Georgia. The four of us had visited Lake Oconee in 2019 and had all agreed it was our favorite trip ever. Something about being on the water, access to boats and jet skis, and the overall vibe made it our favorite, even over beach vacations.

Our expectations were high when we decided to go back, this time with my parents and my sister joining us. We rented a beautiful house with plenty of space and privacy for everyone. We had a boat lined up for the whole week and were headed to the same area of the lake where we had vacationed before. We were all excited and hopeful for a fun week away.

Unfortunately, the trip turned out to be a total bust for many reasons. It was rainy and cold for most of the week, making boating more of a chore than a relaxing day on the water. Many of the restaurants were either closed or not open to renters (only the owners of the property could dine in), due to remaining Covid restrictions. And a catalytic incident occurred that forever changed the trajectory of Josh's and my marriage.

Unbeknownst to us when we met, Josh and I were both two broken people. And we fit together perfectly, as long as we kept things fairly superficial and high-energy. Before kids, we spent a lot of time out with friends, which included many late nights. The lifestyle was fun. We worked hard and played harder. We traveled, went to weddings, grew our careers, and laughed a lot. And drank a lot. But back-to-back babies changed that. Mason was born in August 2009, and our daughter Isla, eighteen months later, in February 2011. Inevitably, babies change the dynamics in any partnership. Some couples weather those changes beautifully—growing in their bond and strength as a couple, while others, like us, begin to fall further and further apart from each other.

I understand now that I picked men who were emotionally unavailable. I did this because I was emotionally unavailable. I didn't know how to be vulnerable, and I didn't know how to draw vulnerability out of Josh. I didn't know how to be close with Josh, and he didn't know how to be close with me. We numbed ourselves with alcohol, partying and friends, and pushed our demons to the side. And sometimes, mostly when alcohol was involved, those demons would come out in a bad way.

On the second to last night in Georgia, some of Josh's demons reared their ugly head. His demons came out in anger and rage, though fortunately not in physical form. Our kids were frightened. My parents were frightened. I was frightened, although I had become used to it and already limited how much I drank, mainly so I could better respond in case it became "one of those nights." Over the years, I had learned how to anticipate and safeguard myself and the kids during these kinds of nights. Sadly, I spent many birthdays and friends' weddings in threat mode, waiting to decide if I would fight, flight, or freeze.

I don't blame Josh for his demons. Most people have generational trauma and learned behaviors from childhood, and I understood this about him. But I was very hurt for a very long time about the fact that he didn't choose a path that included confronting that trauma; it very much felt like he chose his demons over me.

That night in Georgia, as things settled down and my mom, sister, and I were able to get the kids to sleep, my mom hugged me, looked me in the eye, and said, "Honey, I totally get it if you need to leave."

I don't remember if I cried or not. Probably not. By that time, I was so emotionally frozen, it was nearly impossible for me to shed tears. All the years of a marriage when we were unable to meet each other's needs had taken a toll on both of us. And both Josh and I knew then that our marriage was over. Now, it was just a matter of garnering the courage, strength, and wherewithal to actually separate.

Chapter 23

Boundaries

"If you have yet to be called an incorrigible, defiant woman, don't worry. There is still time."
—Dr. Clarissa Pinkola Estés

IN SOME WAYS, LIFE quickly sped up after Georgia, and in other ways, it almost stalled. Josh and I had decided on that last day in Georgia that we would get a divorce. We arranged for our kids to sleep at friends' houses the following Friday night and made plans to discuss next steps.

We ordered in sushi and very matter-of-factly decided how we were going to separate our lives. It was unemotional and pragmatic, much like our day-to-day marriage had been for the previous decade. We were fair, we were kind, and overall, we did it with love.

The next morning, I had to drive an hour and a half south to Colorado Springs to get my second Covid vaccination. It was still that time when appointments were few and far between. During the drive, I blasted music and sang at the top of my lungs. It was like my body needed the release from the emotion of the previous week. But, because I was so numb, mentally I hadn't been able to let it out.

As I was driving back from the Springs, I cried. I was terrified and couldn't fathom a world where I had my children part-time. The thought of it was awful and nearly broke me, just thinking about it. What if they were sick in the middle of the night? What if they were scared? What if they just needed their mom? I couldn't do it.

I got home that day and said to Josh I didn't want to be a 50/50 mom. He said he didn't want to be a 50/50 dad, and so, just like that, we went back to exactly how things were before. We never talked about Georgia again. We acted like everything was fine and nothing had ever happened. We hung out with friends and showed up as one big, happy family. Deep down, I was miserable.

My brain never stopped. I was torn between what I knew I needed and wanted and what I thought was best for my kids. It was literally torture. All day, every day, my brain bounced back and forth between the duality of the situation. Leave and become a part time mom. Or stay and be unhappy in a marriage where neither partner was happy.

Josh told me he was fine to stay like this, in this situation, forever. A lot of the time, we get so comfortable with what we have and are used to that the fear of change is debilitating.

My girlfriends whom I played pickleball with had been talking about an author and podcaster named Glennon Doyle for some time, and after that Georgia trip, I finally decided to pick up her book, *Untamed*. I learned a lot from it about being strong, finding your truth, and choosing yourself, even if it meant disappointing other people. A couple years later, when Josh and I would finally activate on one of the biggest decisions of our lives, I read, and reread, Glennon Doyle's chapter where she and her husband told their kids that they were separating.

"We can do hard things," and "Our hearts are broken today, but in time, they will heal," became my mantras.

The other thing that stood out to me from *Untamed* was Glennon's ability to set boundaries. Although my mentors and I had been talking about boundaries for some time, setting them for myself was something I struggled with. But as I began to grow in my sense of self and trust myself more, which included listening to the gut feelings I had pushed away for so long, I became more confident in setting boundaries and establishing limits where I was no longer comfortable.

Over the years, a very important familial relationship of mine had eroded. Covid had exacerbated the erosion, and the relationship was hanging on by a thread. This family member refused to see any of my family during Covid, despite frequenting restaurants and hanging out with friends during the same time period. The olive branches I was extending were not received in the manner I had hoped; instead, they were met with snark, rudeness, and condescension. Previously, I would have just accepted that it was what it was and swept it under the rug. Now, even though I was hurt and saddened by the reaction, I was aware of the situation in a way I hadn't been before. I was learning that most people respond as a projection of their own inner pain, and not as something I was meant to endure. I let it go and moved on.

When Mother's Day came around soon after the Georgia incident, the same family member suddenly wanted to get together for the first time in over a year, for Mother's Day brunch.

I was surprised, and then I was frustrated. This was *my* day—the one day I felt entitled to relax, ask for what I wanted, and feel ease. Any other day would've been great. But not on Mother's Day, not when our relationship was so tenuous, and everything in my body was telling me that this day would take a turn for the worse if we spent it together. So, I talked to Josh, he agreed, and we told the rest of the family we were abstaining from brunch but fully supported them all going, wishing them a great time.

You would think I'd started World War III. A text exchange with my family member ensued after a short game of phone tag and ended with frustration on both sides.

The biggest lesson I learned from this, and what really made me start to understand generational patterns, was how my dad responded. He called and asked me to forget about the previous indiscretions and said I was making a bigger deal out of it than I needed to. He asked me if I could just make it work, because it would be so nice for all of us to get together.

I said no and became the black sheep.

That day, I decided to stop playing by rules that were established long before I walked this Earth and that I was going to establish my own rules. Rules that no longer allowed for mistreatment or shying away from hard conversations. It didn't matter if these new rules made everyone else uncomfortable. I no longer wanted to live in a system where I sacrificed my needs in order to please everyone else.

That's when it hit me. My loving, kind, generous, forgiving father also struggled with creating boundaries. In an effort to keep everything together for fear of losing it all or feeling the discomfort that comes with hard conversations, he didn't set strong boundaries. I had become a miniature him, and now that I was setting boundaries, finally expressing what I was comfortable with and with whom, it made *everyone* uncomfortable. I became the bad guy, but it no longer mattered to me. It felt good to choose myself and my direct family unit, along with what, intuitively, I knew I wanted on my day. And just as importantly, what I didn't want.

I had spent my whole life trying not to disappoint my parents. I was the good girl who didn't make waves, who didn't upset the apple cart. I did what everyone else wanted to do, was easygoing, and went with the flow. Until that day. I didn't feel selfish or rude. I just felt like I had finally listened to what I needed and chosen myself. And boy, did it feel good.

In hindsight, I had been waiting in the wings for people to choose me my whole life, to stand up for me and for what I needed. Waiting to be seen, loved wholly and without conditions. Until then, I didn't understand that the only person responsible for choosing me was me. And until I loved myself wholly and without conditions, no one else would be able to.

Although my decision initially created big waves, it eventually empowered other family members to stand up for themselves, when abuse and intolerance occurred. My one small decision allowed others to say, "I'm not comfortable with this."

UNWINDING PERFECT

Growth is hard. Change is hard. And there are mistakes along the way. I have made plenty and am still making them. But to finally be able to say enough is enough because this doesn't feel right, is the most freeing feeling there is. And there is nothing greater than to be free.

Chapter 24

Shapeshifting

"Set your life on fire. Seek those who fan your flames."
—Rumi

THE DECISION TO STAND up for myself on Mother's Day, 2021, catalyzed a truer and more confident Christine. I started to act silly again, especially at work. I started strutting around the office like Ed McMahon, imitating his billionaire's strut, cracking myself up. I doubt anyone else found it as funny, but I didn't care. I was having fun.

That summer, some very challenging employee circumstances came up. I'm talking mean, bad, cruel things. It was toxic and exhausting and resulted in a complete restructuring of an entire department. Through this very difficult and trying time, a beautiful growth opportunity emerged for me.

The situation allowed for me to reflect on past relationships with male coworkers, and one in particular. He was much older and had had a very long, successful career in healthcare sales. Over the course of our working together, many situations had arisen where we didn't align on strategy. I knew in my gut he was wrong, but instead of trusting myself, I consistently doubted myself and went along with whatever he suggested. My mind convinced me that his tenured experience had taught him something that, perhaps, I was missing. In hindsight, I should have spoken up or made myself the authority. Instead, I didn't want to make either of us uncomfortable.

This reflection made me realize I had literally been shrinking myself, physically, intellectually, and energetically, to not outshine him. And it wasn't just this man. Over the course of my career, from the automobile industry to the healthcare industry, I had encountered dozens, if not hundreds of men for whom I had dimmed my light. I'd smile, nod my head, agree. Be strong, but not too strong. Share my opinions, but not push too hard. Be smart, but not too smart. And be sure to listen to, and laugh at, their stories.

I knew how to spot their insecurities, and it was natural and instinctual to play up to them. Make them feel bigger by making myself appear smaller. Insecure men hide by becoming more boastful, talking louder, and demeaning others' ideas. These actions often make the man appear more confident and more intelligent. Study after study has demonstrated that men who are louder and appear more confident get promoted more, despite testing equal to or lower than their female counterparts. As women, we have been taught to shrink and not outshine. To be nice, but not too nice. Firm, but not a bitch.

This got me thinking about other areas of my life where I had been shrinking. If the real me wanted to strut around the office, imitating an overly confident billionaire, what was keeping me from doing that at home? With my friends? With my family?

As kids, we learn to do a dance with the adults in our lives. This dance keeps us safe and makes us feel loved and protected. As we grow up, unless we learn a new dance, we find people whose steps match our dance. My dance was to shapeshift and conform to others' needs, and I danced this dance well. I would become a chameleon in whatever situation I was in, to not shine too bright, or risk becoming vulnerable by being my true self.

Stopping this dance and unwinding what I thought a perfect daughter, spouse, mother, co-worker, and friend was supposed to be created space for something even more beautiful to blossom. I no longer was waiting for someone else to see me. Similar to when I began creating boundaries, by becoming more me and removing the shapeshifting, I didn't need someone else to recognize me or stand up for me. I was beginning to do those things for myself. The dance I had been doing my whole life now felt foreign and wrong. This understanding both empowered me and saddened me.

This meant the dance Josh and I had been doing no longer could continue. Our dance had stopped serving both of us a long time ago, and I knew, even though we had decided to "stay together," it was only a matter of time until we decided to throw in the flag.

July 7, 2021

I'm ready to be the hero of my own story.

For so long it was "Should I?" "Can I?" "What if it's wrong...?" And now, it's just a matter of time. I'm free. I love myself. I'm bold and empowered.

UNWINDING PERFECT

I know now why I fell into the traps I did. Why it was always "my fault." It was flipped on me, and I was the bad guy. So, I stopped asking. And then darkness. And then the abyss.

You can't come back from the abyss.

I'm strong. I'm going to show my kids strength. Grace. Love. Laughter. And true joy.

Chapter 25

A Message from the Earth

> "Every time you're given a choice between disappointing someone else and disappointing yourself, your duty is to disappoint that someone else. Your job throughout your entire life is to disappoint as many people as it takes to avoid disappointing yourself."
>
> —Glennon Doyle to her daughter, *Untamed*

SOMETIME IN EARLY 2022, Josh and I finally made the decision that we were officially going to separate. What finally gave me the courage to step into this decision, and what ultimately helped me to understand how a separation was better for our children than staying together, was when a friend asked me if this was the kind of marriage I wanted for my children.

The answer was easy. No, I wanted so much more for them. Even as Josh and I continue to love each other to this day, we just were not right for one another. We didn't express love and joy the way a fully bonded couple should. I couldn't give Josh what he needed, and he couldn't give me what I needed. And that was okay. Sad. Heartbreaking. But okay.

We decided I would continue building the new house, and he would keep our current family home. He was kind and told me I could live there as long as I needed, but I think we both knew that waiting until the house was done would only delay us moving forward in our lives as individuals.

For years, we had been living more like roommates and by this point had become excellent coparents. After the weight of the heavy decision was made, ironically, the energy in the house lifted and was much lighter. Any former expectations of what still could be dissipated, and it was as if we were given permission to be friends again. Finally.

Next on the list was telling our parents and our children. Ugh. My stomach still turns today thinking about having this conversion with my babies. Because Josh and I didn't have a timeline yet, we prolonged this conversation until we knew it was closer to the time when there would be a physical change, like me moving out.

We had considered, as an interim solution, renting an apartment and "nesting." Nesting basically means that the parents rent an apartment together and then take turns going back and forth between it, so the kids don't have to leave the family home. It minimizes disruption to the kids while the family is settling into their new reality.

At first, I thought it was a brilliant idea. We could find a nice apartment in a nice neighborhood where we could walk everywhere. But then, the questions arose: what are the expectations for how the family house will be managed, while the other is away? And just as importantly, how is the apartment managed and what are the rules around that (i.e., is the other person bringing people home…)?

Ultimately, we decided to stay put in the family home together until I moved out. Knowing that we would be separating and not telling our kids was the hardest thing I have ever endured. Every day, I felt like I was lying to my children—like I had this big secret I was keeping from them. And truth was, I did.

One random afternoon, I happened to be at my parents' house, and my dad wasn't home yet. I wasn't planning on it, but I just blurted out to my mom that we were getting divorced.

This was an important step for me. As much as I love my mom and as close as we are, we just never talked about difficult things. Or feelings. Telling her meant I had to be vulnerable and risk being emotional, neither of which I was comfortable doing with her.

While she wasn't necessarily surprised, it did come out of left field. She was disappointed, but not in me. Just that the life she had imagined for me was coming to an end. It was sad for all of us. My parents love Josh like a son and would also mourn the loss of the family unit and dynamic we had all become so comfortable with.

I wasn't quite ready to tell my dad yet, but my mom and I made a plan to meet him for lunch at a favorite deli, where I'd tell him. When I did tell him, he was stoic about the news, albeit also very sad, because he was, and still is, so close with Josh. Having told my parents, I knew Josh needed to tell his family, but that it was his journey and his process. He would tell them when he felt comfortable.

By fall, I had a very strong inner knowing that it was time for Josh and me to step forward into the new chapters of our lives. Plus, I could no longer keep the secret from our children. Every day, I felt as if a barbed arrow had slid into my abdomen and was slowly being turned. I became sick to my stomach each time I thought about telling the kids. As a parent, you do everything you can to protect your children from pain, and knowing I was about to be the one to inflict the greatest pain they would experience up until this point was more than I could bear.

There's also never a good time to break such news. The kids had just started back to school: Isla had just begun sixth grade and Mason, seventh. We were in the throes of some of the most hormonal years of our kids' lives, not to mention the messiness of going from pre-teens to teens and all the other middle-school stuff that happens. We could wait. We could wait until the house was done. We could wait until after Christmas. We could wait... and wait... and wait. But for what? An eventual outcome that was certain?

One crisp October evening, the kids decided they wanted to give Josh and me "massages." This ritual of sharing love by giving comforting touch and energy healing started when the kids were little. I would gently rub their little bodies with lotion and coo, "Baby massage, baby massage." As they grew older, the baby massages continued, and we would spend time on the floor of their rooms together, me softly massaging lotion over their young limbs, hands, and toes. Isla, an intuitive and natural healer, started asking to give me massages, and Mason, also very heart-centered and sensitive, easily joined in. They would collect items from my meditation altar, such as singing bowls and crystals, and incorporate them into the massage.

That night, as Mason was working on Josh and Isla was working on me, she said, "Mommy. I have a message from the Earth to share with you. The Earth wants you to know that you are going to be happier than you have ever been."

I was stunned. Silent for a moment. Wow, I wasn't expecting that. I asked her, "When, Baby?"

And she responded, "Very soon."

Tears filled my eyes, and I embraced her, my little lightworker, for delivering a very special message to me. Her message to me meant that it was okay for me to choose my own happiness, and it was just on the horizon.

No, Josh and I couldn't wait any longer to tell our amazingly intuitive and kind children. And so, I reread the Glennon Doyle section in *Untamed,* where she and her then husband told their kids they were separating, I channeled my inner Glennon, and a couple weeks later, Josh and I did the hardest thing we have ever had to do.

Chapter 26

The Tiny House

"New beginnings are often disguised as painful endings."
—Lao Tzu

THE BIGGEST MISTAKE JOSH and I made, when we finally told the kids we were separating, was that we told them in October, but we didn't have any real physical action until after Christmas. I think it was confusing to them, especially since Josh and I continued to share a room and operate the same way we had been for years.

After we told them, I would check in with the kids, trying to get a feel for where their heads were at. One time, Mason said, "It doesn't really feel like anything has changed."

Which is extraordinary, when you think about it. Josh and I had been living such separate yet parallel lives for so long, even our kids didn't feel like anything was different after we broke the news to them. They were both incredibly mature and pragmatic, both saying they only wanted for both of us to be happy.

Isla even said she knew it was going to happen, and my heart still hurts, thinking about this perfect little girl living in fear about whether her parents were going to stay together or not. Once the worst happens and the center of the fear is felt, the pain we actually feel is usually much less than what we have conjured up in our head. I think, for Isla, it was almost a relief.

By this time, we had decided I would rent a place until the new house was complete, and because I was moving out, I felt it necessary to include the kids in the decision of where. This new reality didn't just impact me—it impacted our kids the most, and I wanted them to feel like they had some say in as many decisions as possible.

It was also important to me that, in our rental home, we were surrounded by friends and in a community close to our new home. Fortunately for us, there was a small, two-bedroom, one-bath rental right around the corner from our new house. It wasn't available until December, but the kids and I decided it was perfect for us, and we could wait. We affectionately started calling it the Tiny House.

For me, my only priority was the upcoming Christmas holiday. I wanted to make sure this Christmas was not remembered as the Christmas when Mom moved out. Josh and I decided I would move my things out the week after the holiday, when he was taking the kids back to Michigan to see his family, and then we would slowly start staying in the new rental sometime in January. In my head, January 15 was the target date.

One night in early December, a friend asked me why we told the kids so early, if I wasn't planning on moving out until after the holiday. She was well-intentioned, her point being we had told the kids so early and now they were left waiting for the Band-Aid to be ripped off. She pushed me and questioned why even wait now. Why not just move.

I tried to explain that I wanted to be in the family home for Christmas and how it was important to me that the memory of the holiday be positive. Her point was that the kids were in limbo, and it was unfair to them.

In my mind, it had made sense to tell the kids back in October when we did, and it also made sense to me to wait until after the holidays to move, when my kids were traveling and out of the house. It hurt me to think about them watching me pack up my things and leave.

But my friend had made a good point, and later, I talked to each of the children about it. They both expressed the same sentiment: it was as if they knew something bad was going to happen, and they just had to sit and wait for it. I was grateful to her for the awareness, which allowed me the opportunity to have that conversation with my kids. Having these conversations and subsequent others have, I hope, taught my kids that we can talk about hard things. That they can trust me to listen to them and validate their feelings. That I will always be a sounding board, without judgment or criticism, and a safe place to land.

The lead-up to the holiday was not much different than any other year. We decorated the tree together, we bought and wrapped presents, made cookies, and played lots of Christmas music in the house. We even kept our same holiday traditions—Christmas Eve and lasagna at our house, Christmas dinner at my parents. I did my best to be in the moment, to soak it all in and just enjoy the togetherness. But I couldn't deny the cold hard truth... Three days after Christmas, a small moving truck was coming to collect my personal items and some furniture. This would be the last holiday I spent living in our family home, with us all together. It was a beautiful holiday, and I'm grateful for the maturity and love everyone was able to show.

After my family had left for Michigan, I got to work, packing everything up. It was so much harder and so much more agonizing than I ever imagined. I had been thinking about this day for years, and now it was finally here. As a "take the bull by the horns, get shit done" kind of woman, this was a new experience for me, because it was like I was paralyzed. I had a hard time making any decisions about what to take and what to leave. It was overwhelming, to say the least.

My personal items were the easy part. I was planning to buy mostly all new furniture and kitchenware, when I moved into the new house, so I only needed to pack the basics for the Tiny House. But as I started going through the kitchen, I was so overwhelmed that I had decision paralysis. Sixteen years of a life together were wrapped up in that kitchen, and I had no idea what to do or where to start. At this point, I was still not processing emotion very well and was unable to feel any feelings, except complete overwhelm at the task of packing up the necessities from a life that no longer was.

I knew I had processed the loss of my marriage during our marriage. Years before the separation, when I knew we weren't a "normal, happy couple," I began to process and mourn the loss of all of the things I had hoped for. There were so many times when we could have come back together, stronger, but instead, a small crack became a massive ravine that was no longer crossable. The years went by, both of us afraid and in denial for a long time. I had felt sadness. Then anger. And then, I simply was apathetic. I threw myself into my work and the business, to fill the major void I was suffering in my relationship. Finally, as I started becoming more in tune with myself and started choosing myself, I felt acceptance for the loss of our marriage.

Thankfully, my sister Kerry was there during the difficult days of packing. She is also a take-charge, get-shit-done kind of woman. She was my savior during that time and my rock. I had yet to process the big emotions that come with moving out of one's family home, stuck in a heightened, perpetual fight-flight-freeze-fawn state for years. My body and mind had been unable to rest for so long, as I operated in a constant hyperarousal state.

Both my mom and Kerry helped me sort what to take, helped me pack, and then helped me unpack into the Tiny House. Kerry took charge of me when I needed it most, and I will be forever grateful for that. As someone who had yet to learn how to fully receive, it made me feel uncomfortable, but I was able to let her in a little bit and receive her love and help.

Together, the three of us made my tiny little rental house a home. It was compact and cozy, exactly what I wanted and needed for this temporary next phase of my life. I envisioned the kids and me cuddling on the too-big-for-the-room couch and made sure my bedroom had a king-sized bed, in case either of my kids wanted or needed to sleep with me. I hung Isla's artwork everywhere and lit fragrant candles. It was perfect for an impossible situation.

The kids were so excited to see the Tiny House when they returned from Michigan that we headed over almost immediately. My plan was to ease into sleeping at the Tiny House and be fully settled by January 15. Josh and I hadn't discussed our custody schedule yet, and I still had a lot of items that needed to be moved over. But kids have a funny way of knowing exactly what needs to happen, and in this case, Mason knew how to rip the Band-Aid off.

After we took the quick tour, Mason asked, "Can we sleep here tonight?"

Not fully processing the magnitude of the decision, and instead willing to embrace his enthusiasm, I said yes. We drove back to what now was officially "Josh's house," and the kids packed some things to bring over. We loaded up the car—two kids, one dog with me, one dog staying behind with Josh—and slowly drove away.

I looked in my rearview mirror and couldn't keep it in any longer. The tears and the pain of what was really happening surged from my body, as if a dam had broken, and I let it all out.

My kids, not very used to seeing me cry, were initially surprised and then became my comfort. Isla said softly, "It will be okay, Mommy. You both will be happier."

I tried to turn off the waterworks that had been unleashed from my almost-always-dry eyes, realizing I never again would sleep in our family home, with us as a family unit. I tried unsuccessfully to stifle my sobs and broken heart as we made the quick three-minute drive to our humble little rental.

As we started to settle in, Mason came up and threw his arms around me. Tears started falling from his sweet, innocent eyes. "Momma, I feel so bad for Daddy. Can I go stay with him?"

And so, we called Josh together. He then made the quick drive over and scooped Mason up to take him back "home."

Isla and I hugged, and I cried more, full of the overwhelming guilt I felt about breaking our family unit apart. We said our, "I love yous" and "goodnights," then ventured into our first night in the new chapter of our lives.

Chapter 27

Jane the Virgin

"She needed a hero, so that's what she became."

—Anonymous

WHEN YOU BECOME CLEAR about what you want in life, you most likely will spend a period of time filtering out old tendencies and habits. This means you may be alone at times, when previously you were surrounded by loved ones. By getting clear on the fact that I had stayed in a marriage that no longer served either of us and then choosing to move out, I was inadvertently electing to be alone half of the time.

Our initial customer schedule was a 2-2-5-5 schedule. I had the kids Monday and Tuesday, Josh had Wednesday and Thursday, and we alternated weekends. It was nice, because we never went too long without seeing the kids, but the downside was twofold. It was hard on Isla, who would pack up her entire closet between each transition, which was a lot of work, and I found that I crammed so many social activities into my Wednesdays and Thursdays, I never really got any downtime.

After a few months, we shifted to week on, week off, which is still the arrangement we use today. It works for our family, because our children are old enough now that they can easily be away from one parent for a week or two without disrupting the bond between each other. A bonus is that, through this process, Josh and I have become better friends than we had been in years, and we both end up seeing each other, along with the kids, multiple times a week.

I had spent many years writing in my journals about the potential of both Josh and me finding our own happiness outside of each other. Writing this book, I even came across one journal entry about a future scenario with me sitting next to his new girlfriend at one of Mason's basketball games, where she and I are getting along like old friends. I want that for both of us, in a way we can still hold space and love for each other, even as our new chapters begin.

To fill my alone time, I started to watch some TV. Over the years, I would occasionally binge-watch a series over a long weekend, but overall, my TV consumption was low. Prior to moving to the Tiny House, I just did not have the time to watch it regularly. So, when my mom and Kerry suggested *Jane the Virgin*, a very sweet romantic series, a nod to telenovelas, with endless episodes and seasons, I was in. It seemed like the perfect way to fill my lonely nights.

Never did I expect to learn important love and life lessons from Jane. The short summary of the series is that Jane is a virgin, waiting for the sanctity of marriage before fully giving herself to a man. Although engaged to the man she plans to marry, she inadvertently becomes artificially inseminated by her hair-brained doctor, who happens to be the sister of the man whose sperm inseminates Jane. (Yes, total telenovela plot.) The series is written as magical realism, and I felt the magic from the beginning.

As the series unfolds, Jane becomes stuck in an impossible love triangle, between the man she was originally engaged to and the father of her child. She loves both whole-heartedly and is left to follow her heart—not such an unusual plot line. But what really stood out to me was Jane's continued conviction in trusting herself and what felt right and was right for her. She loved both men, but both men had separate flaws and different capacities to love her the way she needed to be loved. Jane was so courageous, willing to walk away from both, at different times, because the relationship no longer served her highest good. She loved the men, but she loved herself more and, ultimately, was not willing to sacrifice the love for herself for an incomplete relationship.

For so much of my life, I had sacrificed my needs and emotional well-being for others. Perhaps for fear of abandonment. Perhaps, I had tried at some point to express my needs and, after being shut down, didn't feel safe to express them anymore. Perhaps, I didn't even know what my needs were, and therefore it was impossible for me to ask or choose myself. For all of these reasons, I had settled for incomplete, not whole relationships.

By this point, I had spent many years with mentors like Tammy, Zoe, and Davie, but I had not been in traditional talk therapy since I was eighteen, when Bear died. In January 2023, I began therapy with an incredible human, Thomas Long. Tom was in his mid-seventies, had served as a priest in the Episcopal Church for forty-eight years, and was a psychotherapist. He was the therapist to a good friend of mine, and as he was planning to retire from his practice in mid-June 2023, he only took me on as a client because of our shared love for our mutual acquaintance.

Yet again, a very special mentor came into my life who would leave a forever mark on me. Tom was so many things to me, including a confidant, a supporter, a voice of reason, and a teacher. Because of his gender and age, sharing my innermost secrets (although extremely scary and difficult for me at times) helped me heal my feelings of shame and incessant need to be perfect with my dad. Tom was never judgmental and listened to me intently, lovingly, and without penalty. I told him everything, and he helped me to see light at the end of a dark and lonely tunnel.

Tom taught me how to process many things, and one of the most significant was the concept of duality. My whole life, I had done everything I could to stay out of the ambiguity between two choices. Nothing made me more uncomfortable than a decision needing to be made and wallowing in the back-and-forth between each one. Because of this discomfort, I made decisions quickly and very rarely looked back at them. (The exception being the decision to separate from Josh, which I very uncomfortably sat in for years, because I couldn't risk making the wrong decision and didn't trust my gut enough.) I forged forward no matter what, without regret, and only course-corrected when needed.

In some aspects of my life, this served me very well, such as academically and professionally. But when it came to matters of the heart, I didn't have the muscle memory to know how to manage them and how to navigate the ambiguity of feelings. So instead, I pushed them away or made decisions to move on from the feeling as quickly as possible.

Tom taught me about the tension of the opposites. How holding that tension can be quite powerful, and that dualistic systems always fail. Jane the Virgin's love for the two men was a tension of opposites–her love for both could exist at the same time. My love for Josh, while understanding our relationship had run its course, was a tension. Both could exist. Both had value.

I needed to learn how to maintain who I was, or who I was becoming, in oppositional positions. The key is emotional choice. Am I consciously taking care of myself in a way so that I am free to make choices that best serve me? I hadn't been, and it was necessary for me to begin to rebuild.

Having spent years in an unbonded marriage, while throwing myself into the work of building a business, my friendships had gone unnurtured. I also had stopped drinking regularly somewhere along the way, maybe 2018 or 2019. I no longer could support a lifestyle of drinking one to three glasses of wine or other alcoholic beverages regularly, especially during the week. Getting a good night's sleep and waking up to perform optimally in a business that could go to zero at any minute was priority number one. I needed to be sharp, and I needed to perform at the next level each and every day. The business counted on me, and our employees counted on me.

This meant saying no to a lot of regular social get-togethers we had routinely come to love, with neighborhood family friends. This group of friends is a truly special group, both husbands and wives all getting along exceptionally well and having a lot of fun, and our kids, despite an age range spanning almost ten years, all love and care for one another. The years we spent traveling together, holding spur-of-the-moment dinners, and enjoying evening soirees were magical, and I look back on them with a great deal of fondness.

Saying no meant losing a piece of myself, an identity that had formed that was comfortable and felt homey. I had a social structure, a belonging, a place in the world—which, ultimately, as humans, we all desire and need. Love and belonging are sandwiched right in the middle of Maslow's Hierarchy of Needs, the pyramid of needs that motivate people. Physiological and safety needs are at the bottom, and esteem and self-actualization are at the top. For me, the need to belong was strong, but my desire to build a successful business that created safety for my family was even stronger.

Betty Friedan, a pioneer in women's activism in the 1960s and 1970s, famously said, "You can have it all, just not at the same time." And I believe no truer words exist. I had spent so much of my married life trying to be all things to all people that I had made myself sick, unhappy, and lonely. By embracing the truths that it was okay to not have it all and that there are seasons to life, I was able to take a step back and prioritize my health, my kids, and the business.

By allowing myself the freedom to say "no," back in whatever year I started saying no to drinking and late nights, I had unintentionally isolated myself a bit from a social structure. As Josh and I grew increasingly further apart, often doing our own separate social activities, the business had become my world. By 2020, my social interactions were almost entirely filled by the company's executive team, the wonderful employees who showed up daily to impact human lives across the country, and endless meetings with clients and investors. I loved my job, and I loved leading a team. I felt empowered, strong, and more capable than ever.

We had raised a Series A capital funding round in Q1 of 2022 and quickly gotten to work, putting that money to use. There was only one problem, albeit a good problem and a natural consequence of a thriving business. We had grown so much in such a short time, the pragmatism of a co-CEO partnership was dwindling, and a fracture in the foundation of our collective vision occurred.

Concurrently, I was working with Tom to understand some of the generational patterns that had been ingrained in me from a young age. I was recalling the memories of a young child who put on a happy face and did the "dance" in my family unit, in order to find belonging or to ease an uncomfortable situation between fighting family members. I had been a shapeshifter, the peacekeeper, and the champion of the underdog.

While these patterns had served me throughout life, they had ultimately led to my inability to form close relationships in my personal life. My subconscious was so afraid of being vulnerable that, to protect myself at all costs, I chose perfect from the outside, but never felt perfect from the inside.

Tom and I talked a lot about vulnerability. My understanding of vulnerability was still not fully formed, and I thought, by opening up and sharing stories and life lessons with Tom and with my team at work, I was being vulnerable. I recalled with him the stories of Jane the Virgin and her vulnerability. Her willingness to walk away from a man (or men, in her case) whom she loved, in order to choose herself. I began to see a correlation; I had done this with Josh. I love Josh dearly and am forever grateful for the life we shared; most importantly, I am so grateful to him for the two beautiful souls who are our children. But if I could walk away from sixteen years of marriage, what else was I capable of?

Tom taught me that the ultimate vulnerability was being able to walk away from something in spite of fear. To walk away from all things I had known, from the safety of the world I had created. And to step into the truth of choosing myself before all else. Because, when I could do that, I would show up bigger and brighter in the world, and I could truly begin to serve those around me in a much healthier and more fulfilling way.

At work, it was becoming more and more obvious that the time had come for the business to have a sole CEO. My business partner and I discussed, and even tried on, several different iterations of our leadership roles for several months. But ultimately, we decided that what was best for the business was a single CEO. I decided that, for my own personal growth journey, what was best for me was to step away.

Resigning from the business was as difficult for me as driving away from our family home on that first night in the Tiny House. My business partner had become a dear friend with whom I had worked side-by-side for almost eight years. Another natural void occurred, and my heart broke yet again.

In April 2023, my business partner and I told two board members I was resigning. We held an emergency board meeting and told the executive team the next day. By the following Monday, I announced to the entire company I had made the painful decision to resign. In an emotional recollection of shared memories and pictures of the eight-year journey to build the amazing business that it had become, I was the most vulnerable I had ever been. The outpouring of love and support, not only from the team but from clients and others, was incredible and beautiful. I'd had no idea the impact I had made on so many people. To have them share their love with me brought me to my knees. I was moved beyond words and filled with gratitude. And I knew, in that moment, I was safe.

As a final farewell, I posted on LinkedIn:

> *Almost 8 years ago, I made the decision to leave the "safe" and chase the "what-if." A crazy idea of what-if we could actually diagnose patients with earlier stage disease. A decision that will, and has, changed me in ways I could never have imagined.*
>
> *So it is with very mixed emotions that I share I have made the incredibly difficult decision to leave Eon.*
>
> *Building Eon with Aki and Muneeb has been without doubt one of the greatest joys of my life, and I take with me innumerable memories and lessons that I will cherish forever. Aki, I am forever grateful for you choosing me to be your partner and for us choosing to stand together and fight. I wish you nothing but the best as you drive Eon's mission forward to make patients healthy and healthcare affordable. I will be cheering you on!*

To the Eon team - I love you and I will miss every one of you! Thank you for entrusting me to lead, and for all of the memories we have shared over the years. Continue to be the best, because our communities deserve it.

And to our clients and the patients we serve, thank you for choosing Eon, even in those early years. We have done many great things together and our communities are healthier because of it! #DefyDisease

Chapter 28

Cocoon

"You don't move on because you're ready to. You move on because you've outgrown who you used to be."
—Carrie Bradshaw, *And Just Like That*

I GROSSLY MISJUDGED the loss I would feel from leaving the business. The business—the employees, the clients, the external meetings, all of it—was my life.

My days, weeks, and months had been built entirely around what was going on in the business. I quickly realized it was also my biggest social outlet. I'd gone into the office almost every day, and whether in the office or not, most days were filled non-stop with back-to-back meetings. In the office, I chatted and laughed with fellow co-workers in passing, loved making sales calls, and enjoyed the day-to-day strategy and operations with my business partner. I felt fulfilled and complete when I came home at night and always loved what I did.

So, when that all suddenly stopped, I experienced one of the largest voids I have ever felt in my life. I was empty. Alone. Without purpose. And still healing from my recent separation from my husband.

There is a saying that the right people come into your life at the right time. Looking back on my life, I know this to be true. Every person you meet, every encounter you have, is a lesson and an opportunity for growth. This trying chapter of my life was no different. After both of my separations (from Josh and the business), the exact right people I needed flooded into my life. The beautiful silver lining to most major life events is that you get to see who shows up for you. And you also see who doesn't.

Both groups are needed and necessary for growth, despite how painful it is to recognize the relationships that no longer serve your highest good. By letting go of energetic pulls who take you away from the focus of where you want to point your new North Star, you allow yourself the freedom to say "no." And every time you say no, you open up space to become a little more empowered. Soon, you start to see who and where you really want to show up for, and you start to build a whole new social structure around your highest good. The people and things who give you energy, who give you life, are where you should spend your time.

The thing I needed most during the first half of 2023 was to heal. Between January and mid-June, I spent most of my days as a hermit. Literally, a recluse. I was unapologetic about it and defended my private time and space. I needed to heal—emotionally, physically, and spiritually.

The Polyvagal Theory suggests that when we, as mammals, are grounded, safe, and calm, our parasympathetic nervous system is at ease and regulated by the ventral vagal complex. We are compassionate, curious, mindful, and present. But as we begin to sense different threats, our sympathetic nervous system kicks in to let us know there is a potential danger. This trigger allows us to perceive the threat and decide if it needs to be acted upon or not. If acted upon, the sympathetic nervous system regulates fight-or-flight. But as the perceived threat increases, our parasympathetic nervous system kicks back in, this time regulated by the dorsal vagal complex. This is the freeze response. As any threat or arousal increases, the nervous system increases its response.

The Polyvagal Theory color-codes each response: safety and no threat are green, slight arousal and increase in threat are yellow, and finally, shutting down or freezing is red. During those reclusive months, I realized I had been operating in such a state of red and heightened yellow, my body was broken. Years of sleep deprivation, burning the candle at both ends, conflict, and pushing myself to be everything to everyone had done its damage.

It was like when our daughter Isla had her tonsils removed at four years old. Those things were so big, she hardly could swallow anything, so she kept pockets of food in her cheeks and would chew and chew and chew until the microscopic morsels could squeeze through. After her tonsillectomy, when she was recovered and able to swallow, she started eating for lost time. I remember remarking to the doctor how I felt like she was making up for the week she had been too sore to swallow, and he knowingly said back to me, "No, Mom. She's making up for her life."

Me becoming a hermit was much like Isla finally being able to eat. For the first time in as long as I could remember, I could lie in bed. I didn't have to be anywhere for periods of time. I could watch TV or read a book. Or write.

UNWINDING PERFECT

The journals I filled during this very bittersweet and priceless time will one day be read, I'm sure. But not anytime soon. It's all still too fresh and too raw. Even writing the past several chapters of this book has been almost debilitating, at times. I've procrastinated and tried to avoid reliving the pain. It took a friend and a song recommendation, played on repeat for hours while I sobbed for much of that time, for the blockage to move. There was still so much pain and uncertainty that I needed to sit with and feel before I could finish these last chapters. Once I began writing again, I felt the pain of both of my separations once more. I needed the music and the tears and reverence to complete this portion of my story.

To shed your old skin, you must first go through the discomfort and disruption of outgrowing the old you. Just like a child experiencing growing pains, emotional growth is painful. Once your life is forever changed, it's damn near impossible to go back to being the same person you were before. For me, I couldn't slither out of my old skin fast enough, despite the pain and discomfort. It was as if this inner Christine had been banging on the inside walls of my body, dying to be set free, for months, possibly for years. I couldn't ignore the banging anymore, seeking the truth of my life's purpose and to more consciously live as my true self.

What unfolded over the next several months is what I can only consider to be a series of miracles. Miracle after miracle appeared, especially as I began to embrace my authentic self and grow in the confidence of embracing the woman I now know I am destined to become.

Writing and publishing this book is one of those miracles.

Chapter 29

Attachment to Outcome

"Once we release our attachment to an outcome, it doesn't mean that we're any less interested in manifesting the goal. It simply means that we're less interested in the fear of not achieving it. We've shifted our attention away from fear because we feel safe."

—Dr. Anna Kress, "3 Steps to Releasing Your Attachment to an Outcome"

DAVIE BLU HAD AN emergency call with me early one Saturday morning in late spring. I had been sorting through so many emotions, I was suddenly feeling panicked and fearful. In my head, I had conjured up a story where I was sure I was losing everything I had worked so hard to maintain through my separation. I hadn't slept the night before and was full of anxiety.

I was fearful and angry.

During our impromptu call, Davie and I spent a lot of time talking about attachment to outcome. I had been clinging to an outcome that I thought I could control. I thought, by behaving a certain way or planning for certain factors, I could ultimately control what would happen in the future. This is a fear-based mentality and something that was hard for me to grasp. How could someone ever be excited for or look forward to something in the future, if you couldn't be attached to the outcome? Aren't they one and the same?

Attachment to outcome was also something my therapist Tom and I had begun to explore, which I'd also failed to fully understand at the time. It wasn't until this moment, sitting with Davie, when the anxiety was so heavy I could barely breathe, that the fog started to lift and I began to understand.

As is the Universe's way of doing things, when you fail to learn certain lessons that you are meant to learn in this lifetime, and when these lessons keep presenting themselves to you, but you don't adapt, it will bring your entire world to a screeching halt. It will shake you so violently and make it so obvious, that you have no other choice than to start paying attention. Clinging too tightly to any one outcome eventually will repel that outcome. When you're attached, you lose.

It is out of fear that we cling. And it is out of fear that we lose.

I had been clinging to certain outcomes because I was so afraid of what *could* happen if these outcomes didn't come to fruition the way I had planned. Davie said, "Okay, so, what if [insert the outcome I had been clinging to] doesn't happen?"

We proceeded to go down the rabbit hole of "what if my worst fear came true" and what would happen next. Oddly enough, after ten minutes or so of chasing the "what then," I began to understand that, even if this result happened, what I was so fearful might happen, it didn't matter. Because, in the end, I would be okay. My kids would be okay. Josh would be okay. My family would be okay. We would all be okay.

We ended the call, and in that moment, I released my attachment to that particular outcome. It was freeing. Actually, it was liberating. I realized that never again could I be held hostage to anyone or anything. I was highly and divinely supported, and at the end of the day, even if the worst imaginable outcome happened, I would be okay.

I soon realized there were other outcomes I was clinging to. As a soon-to-be divorced and non-working mother, I was scared to death I would lose the very house I had been building for the kids and me to start our next chapter in. I had been clinging to the house as a future object that I thought I was reliant on for happiness. Once I became aware of this, I was able to take a step back and examine my attachment to it.

What was my underlying fear? That I no longer would be able to afford it without my job? That we may need to sell it and use the cash for something else? My head cycled with thoughts of how I could maintain my excitement over the house, be engaged in all of the necessary decisions, and ultimately still be okay with the idea that we might not ever live there.

Eventually, I was able to let go of clinging to a forced outcome of us living there, and I became okay with the possibility that we might not ever live there. It wasn't my ideal situation. After all, the house had been designed with such intentionality for both my kids and me. But even if we had to sell it, we would find somewhere else to call home. What mattered at the end of the day was not the house, but the love and joy that was created in the house.

With this transition of thought, however, much of my enthusiasm and joy that had come with building a new home dissipated. Balancing the duality of not clinging to the outcome of living in the house, while still moving forward with the development of it, was more a chore than it was fun. I went through the motions and stopped making my daily drive-by or walk-through. While it took some time as I worked through the non-attachment, slowly, something different began to bloom inside me. Instead of dread, I began to feel the possibility of alternative outcomes.

I could still wish and desire to be in the house and, at the same time, imagine what it would be like to list it. In the second scenario, I would make a nice profit, and we would buy something different, but just as suitable for the three of us. Then, I started thinking about all the things I could do with that extra cash. And suddenly, the fear wasn't a fear anymore. The house was either the place where we were going to live or it was an investment that would have a nice return. Instead of fear and an outcome dominating my thoughts, I was now focused on a win-win situation.

Soon, I stopped clinging to (most) outcomes altogether. I stopped being fearful of the what-ifs. I stopped worrying about whether I needed to find another job or if I really wanted to go be a CEO for another company. I stopped worrying about whether I was capable of boundaries in a new role with a different company. I just… stopped. My mind slowed down, and for the first time in who knows how long… maybe forever… I felt at peace. I was content. I no longer lived in the future, worrying about what move to make when and which person I needed to please. I felt so much love from the Divine. And slowly, my new routine began to take shape.

Wake up early. Meditate. Affirmations. A *long* list of affirmations. Prayer. Prayer for myself and for an ever-growing prayer list of people to whom I send love and light every day. Go to the gym. Read. Write.

Abundance in "love, laughter, joy, health, and wealth" became my mantra, and slowly, the miracles began to appear. Rather, I became attuned to them, present enough to see and recognize them. They had always been there, I had just been too busy or distracted or tightly wound to perceive them.

I continued to ask for the right people to come into my life at the right time. The weekend of my big "attachment to outcome" revelation, I was planning to have a girl's night with two of my sophomore-year college roommates. We hadn't spent any time together in years, and this was going to be a fast and easy getaway.

It was only for one night, and I almost canceled. I had been so distraught and exhausted from the anxiety and not sleeping the night before, I didn't know how to muster the energy to show up as "Christine."

I texted my girlfriends, and so beautifully they said, "Come as you are. Broken. Not whole. Messy. Come as you are." And so, I did.

Before this weekend, I don't know how raw, open, and honest I had really been with anyone outside of my spiritual mentors and therapists. But something miraculous happened when we were sitting together in that room. A waterworks turned on, and I became the most vulnerable I have ever been with anyone.

I shared everything. My pain, my fears, my insecurities, my hopes, and my dreams. Through it all, my girlfriends loved me. They *loved* me. They made me feel safe. They made me feel normal. They made me feel like maybe I don't need to keep everything locked in and away from everyone anymore. That it was okay to share and to "burden" them. That it's okay to open. That it's okay to not be perfect. That I can feel and make bad choices and have hurt feelings. All the things. And, despite it all, they still loved me. In fact, I think they probably loved me even more.

That weekend changed me and will forever leave a mark on my heart. Letting go of attachment and the clinging, being vulnerable and safe, and being loved without conditions, it was truly a gift. And I'm proud of myself for allowing my girlfriends in and for allowing myself to receive. Receiving was not something I knew how to do, and I am still learning, but that weekend taught me the beauty in it and its value to the soul. That weekend also taught me what it was like to be fully supported and loved, to be safe to share my wants, needs, and vulnerabilities. All the things. And I was loved unconditionally in return.

I realized I was wounded more than I had previously thought and still had a long road of healing ahead of me. Having this awareness allowed me to step forward into the world, unafraid and unapologetic, knowing that I could show up messy and not whole, and still be loved. I was far from perfect, and that was okay.

Chapter 30

Healing

"Personal growth is not a matter of learning new information but of unlearning old limits."

—Alan Cohen

THE MONTHS FOLLOWING that weekend were incredibly confusing. My emotions shifted from ease and a sense of freedom to terrified, lonely, and doubtful. Sometimes, ping-ponging between each of them in a single day. Heartbroken and devastated, I completely underestimated how much of my life had been filled by the business, and there was an emptiness and a void unlike anything I have ever experienced before. As hard as moving out of my family home had been, the distance in my marriage for all those years had at least prepared me for that loss.

Nothing could have prepared me for the loss I felt after my resignation. My days went from jam-packed with back-to-back meetings and the reward of impacting patients, employees, and clients, to minimal obligations. If it was a week when I didn't have my kids, I had zero responsibilities. I went from waking up before 6 a.m. every day and literally not stopping or sitting down until 9 or 10 p.m. every night, to suddenly having so much time on my hands, I didn't know what to do.

That's when I began to mourn. I mourned the loss of my business, and I mourned the loss of my relationships with my partners, the team, our investors, our board. I mourned the loss of my identity as a co-CEO. I mourned the loss of not being part of the team that took Eon to its next level. And even though the value I had contributed was inherent and could never be stripped, I mourned what felt like the loss of all of my efforts.

The pain was paralyzing some days. To help cope, I started praying. A lot.

While I am no longer religious, I still very much believe in a divine intelligence that, I maintain, is what religion refers to as *God*. I don't believe there is any one right or wrong religion, and I don't believe the all-loving God I know would forsake anyone because they don't practice the "right" religion. Humbly, I argue, "God" is a concept outside of us, created by man and religion, to try to help our human brains conceptualize something so indescribable that it is beyond understanding.

I believe love and gratitude are the fundamental core vibrations of the universe, and increasing these vibrations, while decreasing the negative vibrations of fear, anxiety, hate, and anger, leads to an energetically healthier mind, body, and spirit. This love, this vibration, this is God. This is Life.

When I pray, this is what I pray to. Sometimes I say "Divine," sometimes "Universe," often "angels," and a lot of the time, "God" or "Lord" (a habitual remnant from my Christian upbringing). And sometimes, all of them or a combination of them. But to me, they are all the same. I am praying to a life-force energy that is more powerful than I am. And at the same time, that energy and power reside within me.

The Divine is within me, and I am within the Divine. The Divine connects me to all mankind and all mankind to me. There is a oneness to it all and a compassion that can only be curated and understood when you are willing to accept you are no different than any other human on this beautiful planet that we are so lucky to inhabit.

Mel Robbins, author, motivational speaker, and podcast host, sums up this concept quite beautifully, especially for those who may be atheist or struggle to believe in a higher power. She says simply, "Trust your life." Trust that your life will take the exact right turns for you at the exact right moment.

In the wake of my resignation and newfound quiet time, my prayers were fragmented, focused mainly on my own pain and grief, asking for relief and the breadcrumbs to help me find my new path. I was unsure of my purpose and next steps and was anxious to find clarity.

It was as if all I could do each day was wake and think about all of the things that I had upended in my life already that year. I had focused all of my energy on other people for so long, I felt selfish spending my days thinking about me. Prioritizing my time, energy, and thoughts on myself was foreign and uncomfortable.

I talked to my therapist Tom about this, because I was worried I was being self-centered. His response was novel and profound to me. He said, "So? Don't you think you deserve to be a little self-centered right now?"

This made me pause. Was it really okay to allow myself the space to focus solely on me? Once again, it was like an external source had given me permission to choose myself. Eventually, I would learn that I could give myself this permission, but sometimes, I still find myself falling into these old patterns. The difference is now I'm aware of it and can course-correct.

In addition to my morning prayer routine, I reinstated my meditation practice. I created new mantras that I would repeat three times while tapping a different chakra, depending on the mantra. "I love myself," while tapping my heart chakra. "I'm proud of myself," while tapping my third eye. "I'm a great speaker and words flow to my mouth easily," while tapping my throat chakra. And a personal favorite, "I expect miraculous answers to appear as I need them."

Miraculous answers began to appear everywhere.

One day, I was out walking my dogs, and I had a chance run-in with an old friend who was out with his dog. He also was an entrepreneur, and not only had our companies been founded around the same time, but we actually had officed next to each other at a co-op workspace in a hip area of Denver.

As we were catching up, we realized we both had resigned from our companies around the same time and both now found ourselves in a similar circumstance, where our free time was aplenty and our biggest problem was trying to figure out how to fill it.

He suggested I read *The Untethered Soul*, sharing that this book was life-changing for him. Given such high praise, I immediately downloaded it on Audible and started listening to it at the gym that day.

The gym is another place where I began to spend a lot of my time. I have always loved working out, and I joke that I'm a bit of a gym rat. Having a regular workout routine is something I have cherished since my days as a personal trainer in college but had given up for many years, due to my chaotic schedule. In addition to praying, meditating, and positive affirmations, I found myself at the gym much more. It became my sanctuary; a new source of social interaction, and a happy, healthy place to escape to.

"The spiritual journey is one of constant transformation. In order to grow, you must give up the struggle to remain the same and learn to embrace change at all times."
—Michael Singer, *The Untethered Soul*

The Untethered Soul: The Journey Beyond Yourself by Michael A. Singer literally transformed how I was processing my new reality. In all my spiritual journey and growth work, nothing has resonated with me so simply and so profoundly. The book contains concepts like "we are not the voice in our head" and "let the true self witness the human form."

This idea that the human brain has an inner dialogue, and if the brain is speaking, then who is listening—this was new to me. Who is the speaker, and who is the listener? Who is our true self?

For my own comprehension, I began referring to it as my soul-self and my human-self. My human-self was the inner dialogue speaking inside my head, and my soul-self was listening to what it was saying. As I began to practice this more and more, my human-self started to make less sense, and my soul-self–my gut and heart emotions–started making more sense.

When my human-self tried to tell me something I'd said was stupid or that it is ridiculous for me not to find a job ASAP, my soul-self would recognize the critical self-talk and intervene. Why was what I'd said stupid? Was I speaking from my heart? Was it how I felt? If yes, then great! If not, why? Why did I feel compelled to say those things? And how could I learn from it and grow for the future?

Singer says, "You are not your thoughts; you are aware of your thoughts. You are not your emotions; you feel emotions. You are not your body; you look at it in the mirror and experience this world through its eyes and ears. You are the conscious being who is aware that you are aware of all these inner and outer things."

Instead of the negative and critical self-talk feedback loop I had created, my inner dialogue became a much more compassionate understanding between the two selves, who deeply love and care for each other. I began giving myself grace. I began *truly* loving myself. And my confidence in who I am and what I stand for blossomed.

I began to realize that, if I spoke my truth and it came from a place of love and compassion, then it was okay if someone didn't receive it how I intended it. If what I said made them uncomfortable, then that was more a representation of them than me. I began to flourish. To thrive. To live! And to find joy and laughter again. I slowly began to emerge, opening myself back up to the world.

Something else I learned from *The Untethered Soul* was the idea of never closing your heart. As humans, our experiences leave marks on our subconscious mind and also on our energy centers. We can literally feel in our bodies when we are emotionally hurt. To compensate and to try to prevent us from being hurt again in similar future situations, our bodies close off those energy centers. Instead of feeling and moving through the emotion, we hold on to it deep within us. Every time there is a reminder of that pain, that initial hurt has the potential to surface.

Singer explains it as a negative blockage or impression that your heart hasn't fully processed and holds on to. As humans, this leads us to shut down our hearts, to avoid feeling that pain again. But when we close our hearts, we also prevent new light and healing from entering. And thus, we create a cycle that never is given the opportunity to fully heal.

Singer says, "Do not let anything that happens in life be important enough that you are willing to close your heart over it." He makes it sound so simple.

As humans, we tend to overcomplicate things, especially when we feel hurt, angry, fearful, or disrespected. Our natural impulse is to lash out or to shut down. Singer doesn't suggest you don't feel the feeling; in fact, he encourages you to feel the feeling. But with conscious witness, where you are observing your feelings and aware of how you respond.

Instead of locking the feelings away and shutting down, you simply feel it and let it go. Don't dwell on it. Don't retaliate. And certainly, know that the other person's behavior is a result of their own past experiences. Instead of replying with a smart comment or allowing the guy on the highway who cut you off to ruin the rest of your day, you simply notice the emotion that comes up and then let it go. It's a simple yet beautiful way to approach any interaction with anybody.

UNWINDING PERFECT

Some days, I'm better at this than others, and many days, I need a reminder not to shut down and close. Sometimes, I find myself closing with little things, like getting frustrated with the person who parked their car in front of my driveway. When I reflect back on it, was it really that big of a deal? Could I have parked on the street for the time being and saved my heart from feeling that old feeling? Yes.

But I sometimes find my heart closing at bigger things, such as events or conversations that trigger old patterns and responses. The old me wants to have a snarky or defensive response. And sometimes I do. But mostly now, when I do have an old, patterned response, I can at least sit with it later and come to understand the underlying emotion of what really triggered me. It's almost always something deeper and more emotional than the initial response, and before, when I would be annoyed with myself for acting out, now I just embrace the emotion and give it grace.

This practice has allowed me to open my heart in ways I didn't know was possible, and to share love in a whole new way. On my best days, I share love with every single person I encounter, even if it's just a smile and a hello.

As my heart grows and my sense of self gets stronger, the Universe continues to find ways to share so much love back to me.

Chapter 31

Loïck

"Consciousness is freedom. There is no death, and there is no end. Truth must be our life, because we don't have time for the other. This is life, this is love, and this is truth."

—Loïck Boulmot

AS MY FAITH IN MYSELF and life continued to grow, my trust to receive miraculous answers at the exact right time did as well. I had decided to start saying "yes" to things I would have said no to prior, and I continued to pray that the Divine would put the right people in front of me at the right time.

In early May, Zoe called me. She said something to the effect of, "Christine, you are never going to believe this, but Loïck is putting together a three-month guided program and I'm doing it. I think you should look into it!" Zoe's enthusiasm was palpable.

I knew Loïck from a reading he had done for me in the summer of 2022. He is an intuitive, spiritual mentor, coach and the most grounded human I have ever known. His reading in 2022 was accurate and had confirmed many things my gut was already telling me, but I didn't remember it being overwhelmingly life changing. While Zoe's excitement was high, I was more hesitant.

But trusting in divine timing and relinquishing many old patterns were my new focus, and since I had been asking for the right people to come onto my path, I said yes. And wow, this trust paid off. The three months that followed were, hands down, the most transformative three months of my life.

Loïck is pure magic, and I could write an entire book on the lessons I learned from him during our three months together. Originally from Brittany, France, Loïck grew up with Celtic roots and knew as a young boy he had special gifts. They became evident to everyone in his town the night he fell asleep in the woods and woke up with two deer lying with him, protecting him from the dangers of the dark woods.

His special gifts led him to travel the globe in search of what he was seeking: a universal truth. He came across a one-toothed man who lived alone in a cave, high in the Indian Himalayans, in a state called Sikkim. Loïck was profoundly moved and inspired by this man, who taught him one of the biggest lessons he was to learn throughout all of his travels, despite the simplicity of the message.

Loïck learned, as he puts it, the most simple and clear understanding about meditation and the essence of emotions during meditation. By focusing on emotions while meditating, the emotions create a bridge to remembering and deepening the process. By remembering the greatest feelings of an emotion, such as love, you can use it as a ladder to expand awareness in the present moment. Our feelings are always there, and anyone has access to them at any time. By using them in an active way, one can begin to remember and surrender to one's highest inspiration. So simple, yet so profound.

Loïck now lives in Mexico, and in addition to his spiritual practice, he is a creative musician and an architect. The three-month program he was offering would include biweekly virtual meetings, plus supporting materials such as texts, book recommendations, and his proprietary recordings. In the calls, we would discuss current life situations and have a deep exchange about my inner self. (Yikes!) Over the three months, he would perform clairvoyant readings and subconscious patterning readings, and help me to understand a clearer pathway for my life and its infinite possibilities.

I said yes, and we booked our first session.

Encapsulating the journey that ensued is no easy feat, and I'm sure each client's journey is different. To share what I learned during this time, I've truncated my lessons into four sections:

1. Subconscious Programming
2. Patterning
3. Awakening, and
4. Conscious Creation

Subconscious Programming

Each of us is under the programming of our subconscious mind. It acts like a mainframe and is responsible for ninety to ninety-five percent of our daily actions. It stores every bit of information ever received, perceived, felt, or interacted with, and processes this information unconsciously at very high speeds.
We go into autopilot and perform acts all day long, like driving a car, brushing our teeth, eating, and breathing, without

consciously thinking about them. Similarly, our emotions, feelings, and reactions do the same. Every experience encountered along with the outcomes are registered by our subconscious.

Similar to how artificial intelligence (AI) deep-learning algorithms are programmed today, our subconscious creates outputs and predicts outcomes based on our internal dataset—which are our past experiences and stored memories. This programs us to respond accordingly, often without conscious action or intention. Much of our power is under the rule of the ego and/or the subconscious mind and, as Loïck puts it, makes us not fully in control of what we do and how we act.

The ego plays an important role in our lives, but an inflated ego can become dangerous. It can lead to adverse or destructive behaviors, and no one enjoys being around an egocentric person. However, the ego can be helpful when you become aware of it, either through witnessing, like *The Untethered Soul* teaches, or through conscious intention.

I (my ego) was ashamed of, and fought, my flawed characteristics. I would try to push them away or hide them, for fear of not being acceptable or loved. As I began to accept them for what they were and realized my flaws are part of my internal makeup, I slowly became the boss of them.

By becoming the boss of my flaws, I could begin to heal and revert the subconscious programming driving them. This eventually will lead to a complete reprogramming of suboptimal unconscious behavior, allowing ourselves to feel, create, and love more freely.

I realized that the impulse deep inside of me, in my inner knowing, that had led me to leave my marriage and the company I cherished, was so I could connect with myself, to find my own love story within. To finally fall in love with myself, unconditionally. The good, the bad, the messy, and the imperfect. All of it. And it was me.

For a long time, I'd sought validation and love from the outside. But making peace with myself and finding my sense of self are what this time and space had been meant for. Letting go and surrendering to the beauty of life, to evolution, and to how everything is transformed meant letting go of the familiar and no longer accepting the programming of my subconscious mind.

Patterning

If our brains are subconsciously programmed by the events that take place in our lives, then the intergenerational patterning that occurs in family and social structures are the programmers.

I love people, and I love hard. But I lacked self-confidence, self-love, and independence, so my self-worth came from pleasing others and having good behavior. I learned this behavior at a young age from my mom and dad, and I existed by not existing. I operated at a suboptimal level of my true power.

To regain my power, I have had to unwind the patterning ingrained in me by our family structure growing up. By breaking generational patterns and stepping out of that bondage, one can transgress the generation preceding them and change the trajectory for those after them.

By opening myself to different ways of parenting my children and by making hard decisions that don't always seem practical from the outside, I have transgressed my parents. And my hope is that my children transgress me. Parents can often be the eclipse of the moon and the shadow on their children. By removing the shadow, the children can shine. I want more than anything for this next generation of humans to be more conscious, to shine brighter, and to be more elevated than any previous generation.

Throughout my life, my ego had worked tirelessly to control outcomes and to prevent future pain. Allowing myself to nurture my core wounds and to begin to heal, I started to trust who I am, that I am who I am, and that people will either like me or won't. The people who do like me will accept me for my weaknesses, my strengths, and everything in between.

Once I began to embody this, I was finally able to tap into my true power. I opened my soul, my sensitivity, and all things that "I am." This became a toolbox for me to create something bigger, more inspired, and more divine for my life. My soul has inspiration and is my source of power.

Awakening

In Buddhism, bodhicitta is a mind aimed at awakening and is a quest I have journeyed without knowing most of my life. I've always dreamt there is more for me, both materially and spiritually, and have chosen to seek truth over familiar. In order to consciously continue to awaken, I go within through meditation and breath work to uncover my life's mission; to find something deeper and more divinely inspired.

The will is always in action when pulling from the power of the heart, and it's not about acting or an action. It's about the act of going within—reconnecting with the natural impulses and feelings we all felt as young children. There are no limitations, and now, when I have an impulse, my new work is to act on the impulse and let my inspiration speak.

When I was contemplating this book, Loïck encouraged me to listen to the power of my heart, will, and mind. He taught me that, when these three things align with my divine purpose to realize and love myself, I will see the best version of me and shine. Instead of shrinking, I will rise. That how I love will be reciprocated. And I will see that success is not a curse but meant to bloom. That I'm meant to bloom in all regards.

Blooming means stepping out of what is comfortable, the known. When I resigned, I could have become CEO of another company or returned to a life of sales. I could have done any of the things I had done before, which were safe and/or comfortable. But instead, I chose to sit. To be still. To listen and to awaken.

In return, I now have this book. I have a series of essays that are published. I'm healthy of mind, body, and spirit. I have an abundance of love, laughter, joy, health, and wealth. And I am proud of myself. As Loïck puts it, I gave birth to a soulful expression of my life. I have a gift to give, and it is now coming from a place so deep within me, it bursts with joy and love.

I learned that I don't need to see myself as the enemy any longer, and I no longer have to fight with me. I can put it all under the control of inspiration and something higher. This is tricky, because the ego doesn't want to be replaced by inspiration; it wants to control and protect. Yet my soul now speaks louder than my mind… at least most days.

When you are in truth, it brings you peace. Be in peace, and it brings you love. Be in love, and it brings you harmony. Be in harmony, and it brings you wisdom.

Conscious Creation

"Who am I?" was a question Loïck often asked me.

Initially, I wanted to answer, "I am Christine. I am a woman. I am a mother of two beautiful beings." My mind wanted to relay all of the physical attributes of my life. But who am I is something more. It's not an intellect, a concept, a noun, a verb. It's a seed, one that can be nurtured, take shape, change courses, bloom, and thrive. I am under the power of the heart, the will, and the mind.

"I am life, consciously."

I overcomplicated everything—always looking around every corner, as if there was something more to find or be revealed. Yet all is here and now, and I am complete as I am. I have always been that way and always will be. I need not dwell on the past, as it is dead, and I need not live in the future, as it does not yet exist. In the present, I go into my peace, inspiration, creativity; and love follows.

By consciously connecting with my inner guide, those gut rumblings I often suppressed, my inner knowledge and highest self were made free. Inspiration was suddenly knocking on every door, and creativity was my key to finding out who I truly am.

Consciousness is the freedom to break old patterns and programming and to create a soulful life. When in peace, the heart's desires become accessible. I can laugh, feel joy, be present, create, dance, be silly. I can become wiser. I can love and be loved.

CHRISTINE CLYNE-SPRAKER

I have the ability to consciously create whatever it is I want to bring into my world. With this power, I choose to stop the old patterns. I choose to create new ones. And I choose me.

Chapter 32

Metamorphosis

"I am deliberate and afraid of nothing."

—Audre Lorde

MY JOURNEY TO STEP into my true self has taken years, and many people have helped to fuel my inner courage to do so along the way. But only I could take the steps required to cross over the line and truly become my authentic self. The work was hard and often tireless. But the reward has been beyond imagination.

Setting boundaries was the start of my evolution. It allowed me to express what I was okay with and what I wasn't. Even when those boundaries made me the black sheep or isolated me, and I was lonely as a result, I continued to create them. I came to learn that it felt good to support myself, even when it meant disappointing others.

Setting that first boundary gave me the confidence to set more, putting into motion a chain of events that eventually led to my strength to dissolve any relationship that was no longer serving my highest good. For far too long, I relied on validation from others to feel a sense of worth. To prove my value. I was always hoping someone would recognize the effort and give the same back. Through my journey, I realized that was never going to happen until I knew my worth and my value. Only then could I begin to bring people into my life who were willing and able to be loved, and to love, the way I needed.

One year after moving out of my family home, my life is less chaotic, less disappointing, less fearful, and less upended. Despite not having a "real-job," a husband, a partner, or any of the things I thought were necessary to feel validated and safe, I am exactly that. I know who I am, I know my value, and I am safe. What I have learned is that true security comes from trusting in myself. My ethos, my values, my core. After all, decisions are easy when values are clear.

But also, surrendering to Life and to the Universe. Anytime I stop flowing and try to manipulate a contrived outcome, it doesn't happen. What you resist persists. But when you can surrender, to allow universal life force energy, love, gratitude, and joy to flow through your body, you don't need to cling or grasp or resist. You can flow.

And it is in this state that miracles appear. The right people come into your life, and you can let go of others. Gratitude for all the lessons, even the most painful and sorrowful ones, blooms. By allowing yourself to feel the pain and to be present, the emotions can flow through you and transmute into something new and beautiful. Something so vibrant and resonant, you can't help but feel joy. That is the state I desire to exist in.

I'm not so delusional as to believe I won't ever feel pain or sorrow again. But I am confident that my faith in myself and in the divine will allow me to feel peace, despite hardships that are certain to come my way.

For so much of my life, I was dependent and codependent on somebody else to fulfill me. For love, for confidence, for family structure, or to be a badass entrepreneur. For the first time in my life, I am so full of self-love, I've learned I don't need anybody else to fill that bucket. I've learned that love comes from my connection to the divine and to life. The love I can bring into my small little atmosphere each day allows me to exude it back, and in a way unlike ever before. I'm quick to forgive, I'm able to gut-check and be honest with my feelings, and I've created boundaries. All these things make me a healthier individual, and, consequently, a better mom, friend, daughter, and sister.

To those who have claimed to love me throughout the years but said things to me like, "I gotta be okay with it," or "No one else is going to be able to put up with you," or "You're too difficult," or "You think you can just ride in on your white horse." Guess what? I don't gotta be okay with any of it.

I am too much for some. And that is okay. I choose me. And I love me. I am passionate, messy, driven, loving, loyal, grateful, gracious, strong, soft, emotional, ambitious, big, bright, shy, silly, nerdy, joyful, and a little bit of a know-it-all, but totally open to learn, and full of spirit. And *all* of me is okay.

CHRISTINE CLYNE-SPRAKER

PART III

APPENDIXES

UNWINDING PERFECT

CHRISTINE CLYNE-SPRAKER

Chakra and Visualization Meditation

"I meditate so that my mind cannot complicate my life."
—Sri Chinmay

MEDITATION CAN BE practiced through a variety of techniques, such as mindfulness, guided meditation, breathwork, visualization, yoga, focused, and the list goes on and on. The common goal of all meditation is to train attention and bring awareness to one's actions. When practiced regularly, this can help to achieve clarity, emotional stability, and in general, to create a calmer state of being.

What follows is a step-by-step "How-To" of the first Chakra and Visualization Meditation technique I learned in 2004. The steps are designed to build upon each other. Take several days to learn each step, and don't layer on the next step until you feel comfortable and at ease with the previous step(s). After you feel comfortable with Step 1, then practice Step 1 + Step 2 for several days. Next, practice Step 1 + Step 2 + Step 3 for several days, and then finally, Step 1 + Step 2 + Step 3 + Step 4.

Remember to be patient with yourself! Learning to meditate is like any new skill. One of the biggest reasons I hear about why people don't meditate is because they can't shut their mind off.

That's okay! Acknowledge the thought as it comes in, and then refocus your attention back to whichever part of the meditation you were on. With practice, focus and attention become much easier.

Definitions

Chakras

Chakras make up our energetic spinal cord and are wheels of energy within the body that spin when an individual's energy is flowing naturally. Each wheel corresponds to different physical nerve bundles and major organs, and each can affect our physical and emotional well-being.

When emotions and life's interactions affect us, we either cling to the energy or we allow ourselves to process it. When we cling, we harbor the unprocessed emotions in our chakras. This causes our chakras to partially close or stop spinning altogether and can affect the bundles of nerves, major organs, and energetic bodies associated with each chakra.

Chakra Meditation allows for visualization of the chakras to imagine the natural energy of each chakra flowing more freely through them. This helps to remove blocked and unprocessed emotions that prevent our chakras from spinning naturally.

There are seven main chakras that run along the spine.

Root Chakra: The first is the root chakra and sits at the base of the spine. It is associated with basic survival needs and the ability to withstand challenges. Its color representation is red.

Sacral Chakra: Going up the spine, the sacral chakra is two inches below the belly button. It is associated with your sexual and creative energy, and its color representation is orange.

Solar Plexus Chakra: The solar plexus chakra is next and sits two inches above your belly button, just below your diaphragm. It is associated with confidence, self-esteem, and helping to feel in control of your life. Its color is yellow.

Heart Chakra: The heart chakra is in your chest and is associated with love and compassion. Its color is green.

Throat Chakra: The throat chakra sits in your neck at the height of your thyroid gland. It is associated with voicing needs and truth. Its color is blue.

Third-Eye Chakra: The third-eye chakra is centered between the eyes and is associated with intuition and imagination. Its color is indigo.

Crown Chakra: Finally, the crown chakra sits where your soft spot was when you were a baby. It allows for spiritual connection between yourself and a higher power. Its color is violet.

Each chakra plays a unique role in emotional and physical well-being, and when one (or many!) are not spinning properly, energy cannot flow. This can make us feel stuck, lethargic, sick, unhappy, lacking, angry, and a whole host of other ailments.

Visualization

Visualization is a technique used to help focus and concentrate the mind on a mental image. The snapshot can be anything you wish it to be: an ocean, someone you love dearly, a favorite animal, or any image that is pleasing or energetically serves you.

4-Step Process

Step 1: Grounding Cords

The visualization of grounding cords allows us to "ground" ourselves to Mother Earth, keeping us centered and more balanced. Energetically, we are connected to everyone and everything, including the Earth. Because of this, we can tap into our energetic spinal cord (our chakras) and create an imaginary cord from our root chakra that connects to the Earth's core. The grounding cord allows us to picture ourselves literally tethered to the Earth, becoming more grounded and at ease, and helps us release negative and unwanted energies back to the Earth.

When visualizing energy leaving your body through your grounding cord, it is especially important to allow yourself to *feel* the energy physically leaving your body. *Feeling* the energy while meditating is just as important as visualizing it. Negative energies released back to the Earth will be transmuted from their low vibrational levels into higher, more productive vibrational frequencies.

The first exercise to practice is to close your eyes (if that feels comfortable to you) and begin inhaling for counts of five and exhaling for counts of five. As your body becomes more relaxed, begin to visualize your grounding cord in your mind's eye. See it extending from the base of your spine to the center of the Earth, and imagine it connecting you firmly to the Earth.

Sit like this for five to ten minutes. If you get distracted or have other thoughts, simply guide your mind back to the grounding cord you have visualized. The more you practice focused visualization, the less busy your mind becomes and the easier it is to maintain concentration. After you open your eyes, draw a picture of what your grounding cord looks like to further help you visualize it in the future. Spend five minutes or so each time you do Step 1.

* * *

[I remember getting really into this when I first learned Step 1. I'm a horrible drawer, but I drew one picture of me floating in the sky with a greenish vine coming out of what looked like my crotch. The cord traveled down to the ground and was anchored to a patch of green grass beside a tree and some childlike daisies.

We then had to go around and share our grounding cords with the class. Each person would share, and then the teachers commented. Most people drew some sort of tether or cord, and that was it. When it came time to share mine, I proudly displayed my depiction of me floating with a lifeline to Earth.

The teacher first flashed a look of confusion over her face and then quickly tried to hide it with a pursed-lipped smile, saying, "Well, that is... nice?"

I'm laughing now as I write this—recalling how confused I was about the intention of a "grounding" cord. I had distorted what was supposed to be an anchor that kept me firmly planted on this Earth into the life cord that kept Neil Armstrong connected to Apollo 11.]

Step 2: Energy Retrieval

Step 2 brings a visualization technique used to "call" your own individual energy back into your body. Every day, we take on other people's energy while also expending our own. By returning your native energy back to your body, you will feel more at ease, balanced, and centered.

After beginning your meditation with Step 1 and grounding yourself, imagine a giant sun over your head. This sun has the power to collect your energy from anywhere in the universe. Ask the sun to call back and capture all of your native energy that has been lost in your daily interactions. Sit like this for a while, imagining your energy flowing back into this sun.

Maintain the visual of the sun overhead, and see it brimming with your energy. Begin to visualize that energy flowing first into your crown chakra, then through your head into your neck, shoulders, arms… all the way down through your chest, torso, stomach, into your pelvis, and then down through each leg, all the way to your toes.

As you visualize the energy flowing through your body, allow yourself to also feel the energy moving. As you practice, you will begin to naturally feel the energy moving through your body, almost as if each portion is heating up as you visualize that section of your body.

Step 3: Chakra Visualization

Visualization of each chakra will begin to move energy in each wheel, ultimately clearing blockages created by suppressed emotions and unhealed trauma. This will allow the chakra to function optimally.

Begin by practicing Steps 1 and 2: visualizing your grounding cord and energetic sun overhead. Next, begin to visualize a spinning red disc at the base of your spine, the root chakra. As you visualize it, allow yourself also to feel the energy spinning within the chakra.

In addition to being the grounding-cord attachment chakra, the root chakra is also where you will visualize negative energy passing through and out your body, down your grounding cord, back to the Earth. Visualize the Earth receiving this negative energy and transmuting it into another, more positive vibration.

Continue this exercise for each chakra, going up the spine and stopping at each chakra, one-by-one. Visualize each chakra with its appropriate color and as a disc spinning with energy.

- Root Chakra – Red
- Sacral Chakra – Orange
- Solar Plexus Chakra – Yellow
- Heart Chakra – Green
- Throat Chakra – Blue
- Third-Eye Chakra – Indigo
- The Crown Chakra – Purple

As you begin to practice, be patient with yourself. You may have a hard time visualizing each chakra initially or may try to feel energy movement and not feel anything at all. Or you may find that some chakras are easier to visualize and feel than others. It's all normal and just takes time and effort, like any new skill you learn.

* * *

[When I first did this visualization exercise, my little energetic wheels seemed to be spinning in alignment and peace, and I could feel myself becoming more and more relaxed at each chakra. As I moved up to the heart chakra, though, I realized, no matter how hard I tried, I could not feel anything moving in my chest region.

No matter what I did or how hard I focused, I couldn't seem to get that wheel to spin. In this very first meditation, I uncovered a blockage in my heart. I didn't know what it meant or why I couldn't visualize the chakra spinning at the time.

Eventually, with much meditation and practice, I was able to finally open my heart chakra back up. Over the next twenty years, I would feel it close on and off again, and eventually I recognized it as a sign of hurt or unprocessed emotions that my body was physically holding on to.]

Step 4: Harnessing Earth and Universal Energies

Step 4 begins again by building upon the previous weeks' lessons. After practicing Steps 1, 2, and 3, Step 4 teaches to harness Earth and Universal energies. After grounding yourself, bringing lost energy back, and visualizing each chakra spinning, Step 4 is to imagine Earth's energy entering your body through the soles of your feet and Universal energy entering your body through your crown chakra.

To start, sit with your feet firmly planted on the ground. Imagine a source opening in the soles of your feet, and Earth's energy beginning to flow through them and up into your legs to the Root Chakra.

Earth's energy is symbolized by light-brown, but if you find a different color appearing, as you visualize the energy entering your body, that's okay. The feeling and visualization are more important than strict rules.

Once Earth's energy reaches the root chakra, imagine it mixing with the red energy of the chakra, adding strength to the spinning wheel. Repeat the process with the sacral chakra and the solar plexus chakra. Imagine Earth's energy combining with the yellow energy of the sacral and the orange energy of the solar plexus. By mixing Earth's powerful energy with the energy in each chakra, you clear unwanted and negative energy from that chakra and can imagine that negative energy leaving your body through your root chakra and into your grounding chord.

The three lower chakras connect us to the physical plane, and the three upper chakras connect us to the spiritual plane. The heart is the medium that connects the lower to the upper.

After visualizing Earth's energy in each of the lower chakras, begin to imagine a beam of bright-white light shining down from the sky, streaming into the crown chakra. This is Universal energy and can represent many different things, based on your belief system: the energy of God, unconditional love, truth, a higher vibrational power, etc.

As you imagine the beam of light flowing into the crown chakra, begin to integrate Universal energy into the crown chakra's violet energy. Allow blockages to move and the chakra to spin.

Repeat this process with each of the remaining chakras, including the heart and the lower three. End your meditation by visualizing the closure of your Earth energy source in your soles and your divine energy source through the crown chakra. Breathe in and out, saying "thank you" and "with gratitude" to your higher being (or higher self).

Open your eyes, and enjoy the relaxation throughout your body.

Stay as long as you want in meditation, and do this meditation as often as you want.

HEARTMATH™

"Core heart feelings—including appreciation, care, compassion, nonjudgment, and forgiveness—are very potent."
—Doc Childre, *The HeartMath Solution: The Institute of HeartMath's Revolutionary Program for Engaging the Power of the Heart's Intelligence*

NEXT TO ENLIGHTENMENT, the emotion of love and gratitude have the highest vibrational frequency of any emotion. HeartMath™ is a system created to focus attention on these emotions to intentionally increase personal energetic vibrational levels. Doc Childre founded HeartMath and the HeartMath System back in 1991, and today, there is an entire institution organized around the technique and theory of it. I learned the technique described below from Tammy, back in 2015.

HeartMath focuses on bringing the heart into alignment with our mind and emotions, so there is coherence between them. The most basic technique is to recall a memory where you felt extreme love or appreciation, and then focus your concentration on that memory.

Inhale for five counts while visualizing and feeling that memory of love and appreciation. Exhale for five counts while breathing out lower vibrational emotions, like anger, fear, and frustration. Continue to repeat the visualization and breathing exercise in tandem for five to ten minutes.

Allowing feelings of love and gratitude to percolate through your body will naturally raise your energetic vibrational level. As in meditation, you must *feel* the emotion of love or gratitude deep within you, in order to create this shift. That's why it's so important to recall a memory where you felt either emotion vehemently. Feeling the emotion is what brings the higher vibrational level to your physical form. Studies have demonstrated that the energy of thoughts only travel energetically about two inches from the body. In contrast, the energy of emotions will travel closer to ten feet from the body.

As you focus on the recalled memory, allow your heart to well up with love and gratitude. You may experience a variety of emotions, including tears, laughter, and other physical expressions. These reactions are all normal and natural ways for your body to release stored energies.

When you integrate HeartMath into a practice, you literally are shifting the energetic field that you emit. Like attracts like. The higher your energetic-field frequency is, the higher-frequency people you will find yourself surrounded by.

Exercises in Self-Discovery

"Transformation of any kind always exacts a holy tussle. The newborn butterfly struggles to open its wings, so it can conjure up the strength to fly. So, too, with artists, inventors, mystics, and entrepreneurs."

—Tama Kieves

DAVIE EMAILED ME HOMEWORK following my initial session with her in March 2020. The homework included several self-discovery exercises that I found incredibly beneficial and, with her permission, am sharing here.

In her email she said,

> *I have found, through my own healing journey, that what was most therapeutic for me was the deconstructing of old labels and limiting self-beliefs that had been ingrained into my brain by others and myself. Some had become my identity. To do this, I had to know what those beliefs were. I was in denial with some of them, and with others, they were operating on an involuntary level controlled by my subconscious.*
>
> *Remember that 95% of our actions are controlled by our subconscious. Putting pen to paper in whatever way*

that works for you can be liberating. It takes our thoughts and puts them down in front of us, so we can acknowledge, unravel, dissect, and heal. It's like fitting puzzle pieces together."

EXERCISE ONE: Future Problem Solving

The first exercise Davie presented was to untangle all of the future problems I was constantly trying to solve for that didn't actually exist as a problem.

Davie wrote, "Write down a list of what you go into the future to preemptively problem solve. Remember, we spoke about your mind and how many thoughts you keep there that you try to compartmentalize. What are these thoughts and fears? What are you going into the future to worry about, and problem solve for? These are not present worries—future worries only. Please put them in list form."

I wrote:

1. My marriage
2. Wanting another baby
3. What are my next steps in the business?
4. Mason and what would be a better school for him in HS—local public or more prominent athletic school?
5. Sometimes my sister—trying to create a new opportunity for her
6. Sometimes my dad (parents) and making sure they are okay post-retirement
7. Sometimes our nanny and future opportunities for her

8. How discovering my true self will affect everyone and ways to prepare (this is new)

To which she answered:

1. Marriage: *Try to consider why you feel stuck here OR the need to go into the future with this one. Why can this not be addressed in a day-to-day, moment-to-moment fashion, or even now? Why are you not ready to make a decision here? What keeps you tied to this situation?*

   When we don't address areas in our life that need change and we hold on, we stay in fear and worry mode. You keep yourself here in fear and worry due to the lack of readiness to make a concrete decision. Understandably so. But there are a lot of moving parts here. Can you further dissect this? What are the reasons you stay and what are the reasons you want to go? This will help to identify some of the constant worry.

2. Wanting another baby: *I would sit with this one. I am not saying that you genuinely don't want another baby from a place of love, BUT I do think there are some void-fillers here. A baby could be a way to avoid other parts of your life that you don't want to address. A way to shift your focus to something that makes you happy—a happy diversion.*

   This is also a cart before the horse. Unless doing this on your own is an option for you, via sperm donor or adoption, it would seem your marriage situation would need to be addressed first. Divine order. It's not that you can't desire or set an intention, but when it becomes a worry, you are draining your energy on something that you cannot at this time do anything about or control. Acceptance vs. suffering.

3. Mason and what would be a better school for him in HS—local public or more prominent athletic school: *How old is he, and how far away is he from needing this? What are your concerns? Dig deep to see what is motivating your worry. Are you projecting your fear and worry onto him? Real vs. perceived? I'll need more info to really help you with this one, but for the now, try to answer what I've proposed. Then, if need be, we can dive deeper.*

* * *

[Side note here, Mason was only in fifth grade when I wrote this! Prior to learning coping mechanisms for my always-on brain, these were the wild examples of what I was constantly thinking about. This now so clearly points to my control core-wound and unease of not knowing every outcome of every decision. Eventually, through this exercise, I was able to have awareness when my brain was future problem-solving and delineate between what was a real problem that needed addressing then, and what was a fear that my subconscious had created to help control. By simply recognizing what was real and what was not, I reduced my mental energy expenditure significantly.]

* * *

4. Sometimes my sister—trying to create a new opportunity for her: *Boy and the butterfly*.

* * *

[As a side note here, Davie often referred to the story of the Boy and the Butterfly. The story goes that a boy sees a cocoon and brings it home to watch the butterfly emerge. Slowly, there is a small hole, and the butterfly writhes in the cocoon to break free. Unsuccessful and exhausted, the butterfly collapses to rest. The worried boy takes scissors and snips the hole a bit larger, and a weak and feeble butterfly emerges, only to crawl and never fly. By the boy's trying to help, the butterfly never was able to gain strength and blood flow to its wings by fighting against the chrysalis of the cocoon. By intervening, the boy prevented the butterfly from flying.]

* * *

Why is this your job? Caretaking void-filler? What about her journey requires you to step in? What is new? Is this your idea or does she want this, too? Projecting? Real vs. perceived?

5. Sometimes my dad (parents) and making sure they are okay post-retirement: *Are they struggling now at this moment? Are they able to self-prepare or do they need your assistance? Did they ask for it? Emotional ties can make being objective tough at times. Especially with*

parents. There is a difference between compassion and taking over someone's life lesson and journey. We can elaborate more on this one, too, after you sit with this.

6. Sometimes our nanny and future opportunities for her: *Again, why is this your job? Boy and the Butterfly. There is a difference between feeling obligated and wanting to caretake and save versus pointing someone in the right direction. We can help, but there seems to be a deeper need here.*

7. How discovering my true self will affect people I love and ways to prepare (this is new): *You may outgrow these people and realize your true wants are something different than what you have been saying yes to. More will be revealed here. Work on finding your authentic self and let this one unfold. You may not really know what you want yet....*

EXERCISE TWO: Labels and Identity Association

The next exercise Davie asked me to do was create a list of "labels" that have been assigned to me by myself and/or by others.

Part 1

Davie wrote, "What are your labels? Write down words that describe you. Do this in list form please. Once you do this, we can unravel, as there is a Part 2 to this exercise."

Examples:
1. Driven
2. Smart
3. Funny
4. Sad

* * *

I wrote:
1. Driven
2. Smart
3. Kind
4. Mom
5. Wife
6. Partner
7. Sad
8. Empty
9. Wants more
10. Perfect
11. Lucky
12. Loving
13. Ride or die
14. Strong
15. Spiritual
16. Hard-working
17. Compassionate
18. Athletic
19. Confident
20. Bad speech-giver
21. Second-guesser
22. Intuitive

23. Intimidated
24. Giving/generous
25. Defensive
26. Walled/protected
27. Co-CEO
28. Wants to be respected
29. Introverted
30. Awkward
31. Social
32. Friend
33. Yearns
34. Healthy
35. Pragmatic
36. Busy
37. Popular
38. Successful
39. Daughter

Part 2

Next, she wrote, "On each of these, I want you to identify 'Says who?' Who said this to you? Did they actually say it, or did they make you feel it? What is your first memory of when this occurred? This is important. These are labels but have any become part of your identity.

Remember we spoke about identity issues with your particular mom. We become the jack-of-all-trades. Are any of these your identities, that you'd be lost without, like the guy on the *Titanic*? (Maybe not to that extreme, but you get my point.) What core wounds do they belong to?

I'll give some examples below on a few, but try to do this for each one:

1. Which core wounds?
2. Is it an identity?
3. Says who?
4. Earliest memory
5. Unpack it. I gave brief examples before.

*　*　*

1. Driven: *Not enough self-core wound? Control, too, maybe?*
2. Smart: *Abandonment? Not enough self and control?*
3. Kind
4. Mom: *What are your responsibilities here? Do you have this all mapped out or are you going with the flow? Are they a reflection of you as a person? If they do well, you are good enough, and if they struggle you are lacking?*
5. Wife
6. Partner
7. Sad: *How so? Sad is a blanket emotion. Break this down.*
8. Empty: *You have a busy life. How so? Break this down.*
9. Wants more: *What is "more" to you? What do you want? Do you know yet?*
10. Perfect: *Did you do this to be loved? To avoid conflict? To be easy? Control? Not enough self? Abandonment?*
11. Lucky
12. Loving

13. Ride or die: *When did this start? Why?*
14. Strong
15. Spiritual
16. Hard-working
17. Compassionate
18. Athletic: *Not enough self?*
19. Confident
20. Bad speech-giver
21. Second-guesses
22. Intuitive
23. Intimidated
24. Giving/generous
25. Defensive
26. Walled/protected: *When did this start?*
27. Co-CEO
28. Wants to be respected *Are you not? Who doesn't respect you? What does being respected give you?*
29. Introverted
30. Awkward
31. Social
32. Friend
33. Yearns
34. Healthy
35. Pragmatic
36. Busy
37. Popular: *A validation of the not-enough self? What does this really give you? Truer fulfillment?*
38. Successful

39. Daughter: *Dig deeper with this one. What did it or does it mean to be a daughter? What did it feel like? What does it feel like? What are the responsibilities? If I'm a good kid, I can earn love. If I don't rock the boat, I'll be accepted. If I am the good one, I will be enough and will not be abandoned.*

EXERCISE THREE: Void Fillers

The third exercise was extremely eye-opening (and, frankly, very hard for me to share in this book).

The last exercise required me to look at my days and my time, to see what I did to fill voids, and what the emotions were when I reached for a void-filler.

Davie wrote, "What are your void-fillers? When we feel not enough or empty, we 'reach' for things to fill us up. Alcohol, gambling, shopping, sex, caretaking, time-fillers, food, etc. What are yours?

"Once you identify them, notice, when you 'reach' for one, how did you feel in that moment—what was the emotion? Why did you need it or want it? Try to track this for a week.

"One example I have is with a client who stress eats. I had him track his emotions/feelings whenever he reached for food when he knew he wasn't hungry. Over the course of a week, we were able to track his predominant emotions (linked to core wounds). When he would stress eat, the emotions were loneliness and boredom. When he shopped it was feeling inferior and unworthy. We were able to link these to the core wounds and unravel."

* * *

I wrote:

1. Work: on my computer all the time. Some is sheer volume needed, and other times is me avoiding being social in the core family unit.

2. Exercise: I prioritize 30-60 minutes every other day, but don't necessarily prioritize one-on-one time with my kids.

3. Meditation: same as exercise.

I don't know why I don't fill my voids more with my kiddos. They bring me more joy and happiness than anything. Sometimes, it's the energy needed, and other times, I just don't know what to do or how to interact with them

* * *

To which she wrote: "Great work. Giving you some things to ponder and consider below in italics. Remember that you have your own wisdom, and it's my job to help you find it! I think you'll start to uncover some additional void-fillers, too, as your awareness increases."

1. Work: on my computer all the time. Some is sheer volume needed, and other times is me avoiding being social in the core family unit. *We use void-fillers or reach for them when our core wounds are triggered. When you head to your computer, try to see in that moment what just triggered you. What emotion are you trying to prevent yourself from feeling, by turning to a void-filler instead of dealing with it? Try to track this over a week or so. When*

you *"reach" for the void-fillers, what is happening for you at that moment? What are you avoiding? What are your triggers?*

2. Exercise: I prioritize 30-60 minutes every other day, but don't necessarily prioritize one-on-one time with my kids. *This isn't necessarily a void-filler, but let's stay with this one. Why do you not prioritize time with your kids? Is it something you want to do but don't? Why?*

3. Meditation: same as exercise. *Is this a void-filler or a balancer for you?*

I don't know why I don't fill voids more with my kiddos. They bring me more joy and happiness than anything in this world. Sometimes, it is the energy needed, or I just don't know what to do, or how to interact with them. *Which books did you get about your relationship with your mom]? I think you said you did. I'm going to send you some good ... book options.*

People who sometimes may have some learned behaviors from having a loved one or parent with certain tendencies can learn to detach when they feel stress, fear, or worry coming on. Or loss of control. Sometimes, when the kids are struggling, the parent detaches in a way. I think you'll find some clarity in this one from reading, but I think, for our next in-person or phone session, we can dive deeper into this. Try to track your emotions as they relate to your kids....

* * *

Sharing this: such personal introspection into my heart, my mind, my soul; my failures as a parent; failing in general... Well, it's difficult. It's scary. But I'm doing it because I'm hopeful that, by being vulnerable and by sharing all this, it might resonate with someone reading it. That someone might think, hey, I have some of those same feelings or thoughts, too. And I'm sharing this because I want you to know you are not alone, and there are tools and pathways to heal. Ultimately, though, you must be willing to face your own demons and do the work.

The work is not easy. In fact, it's painful. Dreadful. Exhausting. Seemingly never-ending. You uncover events and feelings you have subconsciously hidden, to protect yourself from the pain. You cry, you get mad, you look at relationships differently. You start to create boundaries. You make decisions you never thought you were courageous enough to make.

But by doing the work, you begin to free yourself. Bit by bit, piece by piece. You stop giving control to others. You start standing up for yourself. You start to realize you are more than enough. That you are more than capable. And that you are wise.

Despite the pain of the journey, finding "you" is the most beautiful gift you can give yourself.

The journey is far from over, but this is me unwinding perfect.

Acknowledgments

WRITING THIS BOOK brought a lot of changes. It opened my heart and mind to possibilities I never before contemplated and has fast-forwarded my unwinding. As I was sitting on my couch one summer day in 2023, cathartically writing, I thought to myself, "I could do this the rest of my life and be happy." As I had this realization, this book poured out of me. I'm not closing the door to future possibilities, but I see the world very differently today. Through this new lens, I'm excited to create my second overture, both professionally and personally.

What I did not expect from this book was the integration and embodiment that resulted. The woman on the cover of this book is not someone I knew when I started to write. While she always lived within me, I worked really hard to make sure she didn't shine.

"Don't be too much."

"Don't overshadow."

"Don't make them uncomfortable."

This was the narrative that ran through my head. I could be smart, or I could be beautiful. On very few occasions, and with very few people, could I be both. To Samantha Joy, you showed me true embodiment at Fempowered Live, when you stepped into your highest self and onto that stage. I'm humbled and grateful for your support, kindness, coaching, and encouragement through the publishing process. Your ascension is a testament to how being brave, making hard choices, and listening to your inner impulse will never lead you astray.

And to Brittany Barcellos, dang girl. You embody fierce feminine and owning your destiny. I am grateful for the spark you lit in me. Thank you for your creative vision, wild ideas, and bringing me in. I loved every minute I worked with both of you women, and the *Unwinding Perfect* cover photo shoot was the icing on the cake.

To my beautiful children, Mason and Isla. You light up my world and the lives of all those around you. Don't ever dim your light, no matter how bright you shine. You both have shown such courage and fortitude the past several years, and I'm sorry, because I know it hasn't been easy. My hope is that you, too, will forge a path that includes sometimes making hard choices, even when it means disappointing others. You deserve a life full of adventure, love, and memories. Remember, you are never too much, and you are always enough.

To my parents and Kerry. I'm sure it was not easy at times reading this book. My hope is, while it may bring about uncomfortable feelings and conversations, we can all begin to heal through it. It's never too late to start the journey. Change is painful, but that's okay. We can do hard things. If anyone is judging us because of it, let them. That just means they have yet to start their own journey. I love each of you without conditions.

To Josh, I wish we could have written a different story together, but I am grateful for your friendship today and the years we spent together. Our children are the biggest gift, and I thank you for that. To Aki, you believed in me before I did. Thank you for choosing me to be your partner and the opportunity we created for both of our families.

To all of the people who showed up *big* for me in 2023, *thank you*. To those who texted, kept in touch, checked in—thank you. Jen, you've been my ride or die for thirty-plus years. Thank you. Abbey, Kelly, Sara and Sarah, you have loved me at every stage and age. #3005Dartmouth for life. Thank you. Emily, your balance and wisdom is helping me jump off that roof and I am grateful for you and you grounding energy. Thank you. Kim, you went first and taught me the do's and don'ts. And gave me a kick-ass house. Thank you. Colin, the universe knew exactly what it was doing when it gave me that upgrade. You have profoundly changed my world. Thank you. Karen and Erin, you came back into my life at the most precious of times, and I will never let you go again. Thank you. Assssssspen! Tina and Michelle, I'm grateful for our sisterhood and shared experiences. You made a very tough year less tough. Thank you. And Bo! "Welcome back," he said. Heck yeah, we on. Thank you.

To all of my mentors, many of whom were mentioned in this book, thank you. This journey would not have happened without you. Loïck, you have helped to unlock my inner knowing, and there is no going back. And *thank you* for the beautiful foreword. To Pamela, whom I did not write about, my hope is that I have the courage to share our experiences one day. Thank you for all of your love and support.

Finally, to the people kind enough to read the first edit: Jen, George, Ben, and Jenn. You made it safe for me to be vulnerable, and I'm forever grateful. Having you read the first draft was beyond scary, but your feedback was necessary for the book to evolve the way it did. Thank you all.

I am humbled and honored by anyone who chooses to pick up this book and read it. Thank you. My hope is that something inside it will ignite your inner impulse, and for you to find the courage to step into the life you desire and deserve.

Christine Clyne-Spraker

CHRISTINE CLYNE-SPRAKER

About the Author

CHRISTINE CLYNE-SPRAKER is a Colorado native who lives in Denver with her two teenage children, Mason and Isla, and two thirty-pound labradoodles, Zeus and Ivy. Christine spent the majority of her career in healthcare on the industry side, specializing in business development and sales for large medical device companies. When given the opportunity to join a friend and help establish a healthcare technology company in 2015, Christine jumped at the chance. This was a life-changing decision and led her on a journey to become co-CEO with the founder. Together, they built a leading health-tech company that has changed lives and communities across the country.

In 2023, Christine made the difficult decision to leave the company she affectionately referred to as her third baby, when her inner knowing recognized it was time to step into the next chapter of her life. Unclear of what that looked like, Christine began writing as a cathartic release, and soon, a book—this book—poured from her.

Christine recognizes her journey was not conventional or easy. But by listening to her inner voice, she accepted there was an opportunity for something bigger than she is. In addition to the book, Christine has founded co-foundHer, a boutique advisory firm specific to entrepreneurs who are on a path to profit *and* enlightenment. co-foundHer is the virtual co-founder for men and women seeking partnership along their entrepreneurial journey. Through Christine's vast experiences as a businesswoman, mom, and wife, she recognizes the imbalance that so often occurs and has founded co-foundHer to support the integration of the material and spiritual worlds. Her intention is to help bring balance to founders intent on stepping into their greatest potential.

For more information, visit: www.co-foundHer.com

To follow more of the *Unwinding Perfect* story, visit: www.unwindingperfect.com

www.ingramcontent.com/pod-product-compliance
Lightning Source LLC
LaVergne TN
LVHW011416080426
835512LV00005B/93